# LITTLE BOOK OF

# ANCIENT
# ROME

Rupert Matthews

# LITTLE BOOK OF

# ANCIENT ROME

First published in the UK in 2014

© Demand Media Limited 2014

www.demand-media.co.uk

Printed and bound in Europe

ISBN 978-1-910270-14-1

# CONTENTS

# Chapter 1

# THE KINGDOM OF ROME

The early history of Rome is shrouded in mystery. No written sources survive from this early period and historians have long been forced to rely on documents written many centuries later. The tale these later sources tell is obviously not very reliable, but there have been long and detailed debates about how much of them we can believe.

Even if the Roman histories written in about 200 BC or 100 BC are taken at face value there are great chunks of the story of early Rome missing. Long years go by when nothing is recorded as having happened at all, which is obviously not what really happened. The later historians also include a lot of information about gods and monsters that is better read as being legend rather than history. This has caused some modern historians to doubt everything that these historians wrote and they declare that the early history of Rome is entirely invented and should be ignored. But such a sweeping statement cannot be true.

Ancient Roman writers such as Livy or Polybius had access to all sorts of historical sources that have since been lost. They could consult the official archives of Rome, which included such things as treaties with other states, the lists of men who had held official positions and financial accounts of the army, road building and other state departments. In addition to this the Pontifex Maximus, or Chief Priest, had the duty at the

ABOVE The first stone
walls of Rome are
erected in about 550 BC

end of each year of writing down what
he considered to have been the most
important events. Those writings were
then stored in the temples.

There were also numerous private
documents, such as family archives,
temple records and business contracts
that could be consulted. None of these
sources would have given a complete

history, and many of them would
have been biased - a family archive
for instance would probably present
ancestors in a flattering light. It is a
matter of guesswork how reliable these
documents were and how accurately the
historians whose work has survived took
information from them.

So with all those facts in mind we

ABOVE The earliest people living in what would become Rome were farmers and shepherds

must turn to the history of Rome as we have it. According to the ancient historians, Rome was founded on 21st April 753 BC by twin brothers named Romulus and Remus.

These boys were the sons of the war god Mars by a priestess named Rhea Silvia, a descendent of refugees from Troy who had fled to Italy five centuries earlier. Worried by the power of such semi-divine babies, the ruler of the area had the two boys exposed to the elements in a wild desolate spot beside the Tiber. The boys were saved by a she-wolf who suckled them and protected them until a shepherd named Faustulus found them and took them as his own. The boys grew up as shepherds, leading their fellows in fights against bandits and organising a form of protection racket to take money from local farmers in return for defence against robbers.

It was with this motley crew of shepherds and strong-arm men that Romulus and Remus founded the settlement that became Rome, on a hill known as the Palatine. The settlement was intended as a base for their military operations. In a fit of jealous rage, Romulus killed Remus and so became the sole ruler or King of this new place called Rome. As king, Romulus and the later rulers, were automatically the leaders of the army in battle. The foundation of Rome had been due to the military exploits of early Romans, so it was natural that military authority should be in the hands of the rulers.

To provide his men with women, Romulus organised the kidnapping of several dozen young women from the nearby farming villages of Caenina,

Crustimium and Antemnae, settlements occupied by a people known as the Sabines. The Sabines were, understandably, angry and sent an army against Rome the following summer. Acron, King of

ABOVE The Temple of Romulus, built several hundred years after the death of King Romulus himself

Caenina, was killed by Romulus but further bloodshed was stopped by the kidnapped women who ran between the opposing forces. They persuaded their fathers and brothers not to attack the Romans, whom they now regarded as their husbands, and peace was made.

These colourful legends were given some credence during building work on the Palatine Hill immediately after the Second World War. In an area of soil previously undisturbed as it had been the pleasure gardens of the emperors was found the faint traces of the foundations of three wooden huts. Archaeologists dated the huts to around 700 BC, a year surprisingly close to the traditional date of the founding of Rome and on the exact spot claimed by the old legends.

Archaeology has similarly revealed the arms and armour that would have been used by these first Romans. Made almost exclusively of bronze, the weapons were long, straight bladed swords used for slashing and heavy spears some 6 feet long. Most men would have had helmets made of bronze and decorated with crests or plumes of varying size. A curious piece of armour which was common throughout central Italy at this time is now known to archaeologists as a 'pectoral'. It consists of a thick square or rectangular piece of cast bronze, covered with circular patterns. This was held in place over the chest by leather straps and would have provided some protection against a spear thrust, though the shoulders were left exposed to a cutting blow. Richer men would have been able to afford breastplates of embossed bronze. Most men carried shields made of planks of wood, usually painted in plain colours. These tended to be round, though some were oval, and about 24 inches across.

These early Romans would have fought on foot in loose groups that lacked any real tactical cohesion. This style of fighting is recorded by the historian Plutarch, writing about the year 100 AD. Plutarch writes that in one skirmish Romulus himself broke through enemy ranks to kill an enemy king, a feat that would be almost impossible in battles between formations of close-order infantry, which became the norm later.

Another indication, perhaps, that the later historians were not wildly inaccurate when writing about early Rome.

When he was 53 years old, in a year usually given as 717 BC, Romulus and a group of nobles were making sacrifice to the gods on the Quirinal Hill when a sudden storm or whirlwind struck. Everyone dived for cover and when the storm had passed they came out again. Romulus was missing. A nobleman named Proculus said that he had seen the hands of a god come down and lift Romulus up to the heavens. The people of Rome declared that Romulus had become a god and erected a temple to him.

Whatever had really happened to Romulus, Rome now lacked a king. After some delay caused by bickering among the nobles, the Romans chose a Sabine named Numa Pompilius. Numa seems to have been chosen as he was born on the exact day that Rome was founded, and because he had a reputation for piety. He was said to have a personal relationship with the beautiful nymph Egeria, who gave him advice about the gods and how to please them with rituals and sacrifice.

Numa is said to have established the key temples and festivals of Rome. He apparently wrote down exactly how sacrifices should be made to different gods and how different rituals should be carried out. Later Romans said that the books were consulted frequently to ensure that everything was done properly to keep the deities happy.

Numa died peacefully in his sleep at the age of 80 in 673 BC. He was followed as king by a Roman nobleman named Tullus Hostilius. Most historians accept that Tullus Hostilius really did exist, largely on the evidence of his name. Tullus is a unique name while Hostilius

LEFT A warrior wearing the equipment of a soldier from the time of the early Roman kings. His helmet and breastplate are made of bronze, the shield of wood and his spear tipped with bronze

### Traditional Dates of the Kings of Rome

| | |
|---|---|
| Romulus | 753–716 BC |
| Numa Pompilius | 715–673 BC |
| Tullus Hostilius | 673–642 BC |
| Ancus Marcius | 642–616 BC |
| Lucius Tarquinius Priscus | 616–579 BC |
| Servius Tullius | 578–535 BC |
| Lucius Tarquinius Superbus | 535–509 BC |

is a very archaic form, so the name is unlikely to have been invented later on. Whether the dates and events of his reign are at all reliable is another matter.

Tullus was believed by later Romans to have been responsible for two great events. First he fought a war against the town of Alba Longa, which lay about 12 miles southeast of Rome. Alba Longa was defeated and became a vassal of

ABOVE The site of the city of Alba Longa, one of the first cities to be conquered by Rome

Rome. Tullus then launched a war against the larger city of Veii, which stood 10 miles north of Rome. During this war Mettius Fufetius, ruler of Alba Longa, betrayed Rome and changed sides. In revenge Tullus had Mettius executed, then had the entire town of Alba Longa demolished. The homeless population were moved to Rome where they were made Roman citizens.

This was the first time that outsiders had been made citizens of Rome. Later generations saw it as a fateful move, setting a precedent for incorporating defeated peoples into the Roman state to make it stronger.

The second important achievement of Tullus was the building of the Curia Hostilia, the large structure in which the Senate met. Historians disagreed about what form the Senate took at this early date, but it was probably a meeting of the nobles of Rome which was presided over by the king. The building lasted until 53 BC when it was destroyed by fire.

This Curia stood on the north side of the Forum and its foundations have been found by archaeologists. The remains were dated to around 600 BC and seem to have stood on top of a layer of ash that covered much of the site of Rome. This ties in with the story that the Senate had first met in an old temple, but that Tullus built the Curia after a fire destroyed the temple. The date of 600 BC is much later than the traditional date for the reign of Tullus. Modern historians believe that the long reigns given to the Kings of Rome by Republican historians are unlikely to be accurate. They think it more likely that

the kings had shorter reigns, so the date of 600 BC for Tullus may be about right.

After Tullus refused to carry out the sacred rituals as laid down by Numa he was struck by lightning and reduced to a pile of ashes. The Senate then called a great meeting of all the citizens of Rome, who elected a new king. The new ruler was Ancus Marcius, the son of Numa's daughter Pompilia and a nobleman named Marcius. Perhaps wisely, the first known act of Ancus was to have the instructions for the proper rituals written down by Numa copied out and opened to the public. Nobody was going to get a ritual wrong again.

It was about this time that two great leagues first impacted on Rome. To the south stretched a fertile plain that was inhabited by a people called the Latins. Latium as the country was known extended for some 50 miles, reaching from the coast to the mountains. There were numerous towns and villages in the area, which were each self-governing but which had formed a loose league.

To the north of Rome was a second grouping of loosely allied cities. This Etruscan League was made up of 12 powerful cities, and numerous smaller towns and villages that lay between the

River Tiber and River Arno.

Rome lay between the two leagues, and belonged to neither. The people of Rome spoke Latin, but much of their culture and several gods came from the Etruscans.

While Ancus was being elected, the Latin League invaded Roman territory.

Ancus responded by mustering the men of Rome for war. He captured the Latin city of Politorium, demolished it and moved the population to live in Rome. He then marched out again, defeated the combined army of the Latin League and captured Medullia, which was made a subject of Rome. Ancus then annexed a

swathe of territory between Rome and the sea. At the mouth of the Tiber he built a small port that would later grow into the town of Ostia.

In Rome Ancus built the Sublicius bridge, the first known bridge over the Tiber, and the Mamertine, the first Roman prison.

During the reign of Ancus a staggeringly rich Etruscan named Lucius Tarquinius Priscus came to live in Rome. Tarquinius was half Greek, and so had been banned from holding any sort of public office in his Etruscan home town of Tarquinia. There was no such bar in Rome and soon Tarquin was one of the most popular and best known men in Rome. Ancus welcomed Tarquin to the royal palace and gave him important positions.

One week the sons of Ancus went out hunting in the Sabine Hills. While they were gone Ancus died suddenly and Tarquin spoke at his funeral. The public assembly acclaimed Tarquin to be king, which understandably annoyed the sons of Ancus when they got home. There were dark mutterings that Ancus's death may not have been entirely natural.

Tarquin moved quickly to shore up his support. He raised 100 new families to be of the patrician class and doubled the families who ranked as equites. He then launched a war of conquest against the Latins, taking eight towns and making them pay tribute to Rome. The Sabines were fought next and enormous amounts of booty were brought back to Rome. The Etruscans, alarmed by the sudden rise in Roman power, attacked and a series of battles were fought around Fidenae, an important bridging point on the upper Tiber. Rome emerged triumphant and more loot flowed into the city.

The actions of Tarquin in enlarging both the patrician class and the equites has engaged the interest of historians. The size and social structure of Rome at this early date is rather obscure. Much later Roman society was divided into classes, each with its own rigidly controlled legal rights and obligations. Their basic division was into Roman citizens and non-citizens. Citizens were adult men whose father had been a citizen, or who had been granted citizenship by the state. Women and children could not be citizens, neither could foreigners no matter how long they lived in Rome.

The citizens and their families were then divided into three classes. At the top were the patricians. These were families

LEFT Only the lower courses of the walls of the Temple of Jupiter remain today, but it was once the largest and most impressive building in Rome

who were eligible to stand for any political office or military command that they fancied. They tended to be wealthy, were often landowners and were most certainly considered to be great nobles. Next were the Equites, who could hold some, but not all, public offices. The Equites were often wealthy through trade or landowning, sometimes more so than patricians, but not always. Then there were the plebeians who made up the bulk of the citizenry. Plebeians were farmers, blacksmiths, potters or otherwise earned a living by manual work.

The plebeians were not allowed to hold most political or military positions, but did vote in the elections.

Because of the complex way in which Roman elections were organised a vote by a patrician was worth more than a vote by an equite, which was in turn more valuable than a plebeian vote. Voting was done publicly and openly so that other citizens could see how a person voted. It was considered perfectly reasonable for a plebeian to cast his vote in return for a job, favour or cash payment, which was why richer patricians tended to win elections and hold important political and military positions. The Senate was composed of men who had previously held certain offices, so that tended to be made up of rich patricians as well.

Outside the families who could claim citizenship were the non-citizens. These were divided into three groups. First there were foreigners who had come to live in Rome. Many of these people were tradesmen or merchants, and some were quite wealthy. They were treated with respect and had some legal rights, but had no real importance. Even less important were the slaves. At this date there were relatively few slaves in Rome, but the proportion

## The Seven Hills of Rome

The Seven Hills that were within the oldest defensive walls of Rome were:

Quirinal Hill
Viminal Hill
Esquiline Hill
Caelian Hill
Palatine Hill
Capitoline Hill
Aventine Hill

would rise dramatically in later years. Slaves were not entirely without rights, but they were few and life was harsh. Then there were freed slaves. These people occupied a sort of social limbo, they had more rights than slaves, but were neither citizens nor foreigners. Most Romans treated them with some contempt.

What is not clear is to what extent this social and electoral system was in place in the days of Tarquin. There is always a tendency for people to project backwards the customs, institutions and morals of their own times on to the past. Modern films or television dramas set in the past very often show characters walking, talking and behaving like modern people.

Roman historians looking back to the years of the Kings of Rome may have been doing the same thing. Just because Tullus built a building in which the Senate could meet does not necessarily mean that the Senate had the same powers that it had later nor that its members were chosen in the same way. Much the same

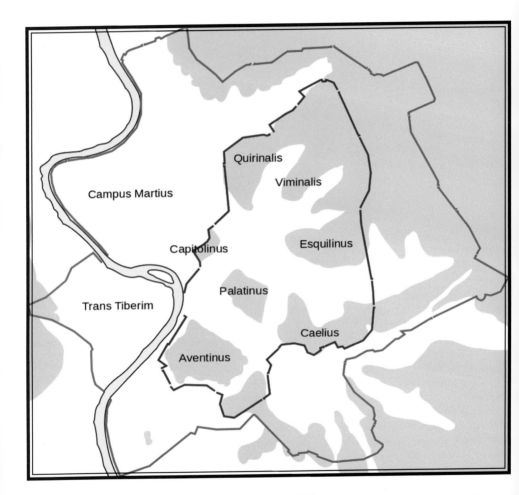

applies to Tarquin's expansion of the patrician and equite classes. These classes may well have existed in royal times, but their rights and privileges may not have been what they became later.

Tarquin may have been doing his best to gain support, but it wasn't good enough. A riot broke out after agitation by the sons of Ancus and Tarquin was carried back to the palace with head wounds. His queen, Tanaquil, announced that he was severely wounded and that until he recovered the regent would be Servius Tullius.

This event is one of the clearest indications we have that the chronology of early Rome is suspect. According to official versions, this riot took place 38 years after Tarquin became king, but it seems unlikely that the sons of Ancus would have waited that long to try to get their revenge.

Servius Tullius was the son in law of Tarquin, having married his daughter Tarquinia. His parents had come from the Latin town of Corniculum and had been brought to Rome as hostages for their native town's good behaviour after it was defeated in war by Rome. The circumstances of Servius's birth are disputed and one version says he was the son of the god Vulcan, in another son of a Roman nobleman.

No sooner was Servius installed as regent than Tarquin died, and the Senate elected Servius to be the next king. The Senate sent soldiers to arrest the sons of Ancus, but they fled to the Latin League for sanctuary. It was, however, the Etruscans who attacked Rome, perhaps resenting the death of an Etruscan ruler. Servius defeated the Etruscans in three great battles and each time returned to Rome in triumph. Perhaps to placate Etruscan feeling, Servius married his two daughters to the two sons of Tarquin.

It was, according to later accounts, Servius who decided that Rome needed proper defences. Previously the early hills of Rome - the Capitoline, Palatine and Caelian - had their own defences. Over the years more buildings had sprung up on the Quirinal, Aventine, Viminal and Equiline while the marshy valleys between had been drained and used as public open spaces for markets and chariot racing. What defences had been erected around these new areas is not clear, and it may be that in times of danger people would have crowded on to the three defended hills for protection. Now Servius decided to surround

LEFT The extent of ancient Rome. The blue line shows the course of the Servian Wall at about 550 BC, the red line shows the course of the Aurelian Wall, built in AD 275

all of Rome with a new wall.

The Servian Wall remained the main defence of Rome for centuries, though it was rebuilt and improved several times. The fragments of wall that remain today seem to date to around 400 BC. The wall stood over 30 feet tall and was built of large stone blocks. In places it was strengthened by towers or ramparts and was fitted with catapults and other engines of war. It ran for seven miles and had 16 gates.

The Servian Wall is interesting not only as a piece of military engineering, but also as an indication of the size and wealth of Rome at the time it was built. We know that the lower areas between the hills were used mostly as open spaces, and that the Aventine Hill was mostly undeveloped, so about half the land inside the walls was not built on. This is not unusual as city walls were expected to provide shelter for farmers from surrounding villages, along with their livestock and goods - all of which needed to go somewhere.

Even so it seems likely that the population of Rome was around 20,000 at this date. The number of citizens would have been much lower, perhaps 4,000. That would have made Rome one of the larger, but far from the largest, city in Italy at the time.

Servius was credited by later Romans with introducing a vast number of legal and constitutional reforms, though how many were really his work is unclear. One of the most important of these was the Census. The population had grown so large that it was no longer possible for people to remember to which social class everyone else belonged. Servius established officials called Censors, who maintained a list of all the citizens of Rome, what their social class was and how much money they had. He also made voting easier, encouraging more plebs to take part in elections. Servius also took the step of moving Rome into the Latin League, which within a few years Rome would lead.

During these years, Servius had shown favour to his son in law, Lucius Tarquin, the son of the former King Tarquin. It seems to have been Servius's daughter Tullia, who plotted what happened next. Having sounded out several of his fellow senators, Tarquin one day entered the Senate and made a speech denouncing Servius as a bad king who had transferred political power from the patricians to the plebeians. The senators, nearly all of

them patricians, applauded loudly.

The supporters of Servius sent a message to the king alerting him to what was happening. Servius left the palace to hurry to the Curia, but along the way he was murdered by a gang of thugs sent by Tullia. When news of Servius's death reached the Senate a group of armed men barged in and declared Tarquin to be king. The senators, cowed by the drawn swords, at once elected Tarquin king.

Tarquin turned to religion to find popularity. Work on a new Temple of Jupiter on the Capitoline Hill had been begun by his father, but not yet finished. Tarquin lavished money and workmen on the project with the result that the finished building was the biggest temple in all Latium. He also fought wars against neighbouring peoples hoping to gain loot for Rome.

Meanwhile, the senate and people of Rome had begun to resent Tarquin's increasingly autocratic rule and heavy taxation. When Tarquin's son raped a noble woman who refused to give in to his lecherous advances a rebellion began that forced Tarquin to flee Rome.

Left without a king, the Romans decided not to elect a new monarch. Instead they chose to establish a republic.

# Chapter 2

# THE GROWING REPUBLIC

Having expelled King Tarquin and decided to become a republic in 509 BC, Rome had two immediate and pressing problems. First it had to come up with a constitution for the new republican state, and second it had to deal with an invasion by Tarquin leading a huge army of Etruscans.

The constitutional issue was solved quickly and easily. The constitution of Rome was left as it had been under the kings, except that instead of there being a King elected for life, there would be two "consuls" elected for a single year. The consuls would share the powers that had previously belonged to the king, needing to agree on an action before it could go forward. It was hoped that this would stop any one man acquiring all the powers of a king. The constitution went further. New officials called Tribunes were put in place whose job was to ensure that the consuls obeyed the law. And the Senate was given the right to send an instruction to a consul, which he would have to obey.

The constitution of the Roman republic would change gradually over the centuries that followed. Most changes were moves to shift political power away from the patricians and down the social scale to the equites and plebeians. In general the internal history of Rome over the next four centuries was stable and change was gradual. Ultimate power rested with elections in which plebeians cast the most votes, but the people

holding political and military office were patricians and equites. It was not until economic problems hit Rome from about 140 BC onwards that things began to change.

Meanwhile, Rome had to defeat Tarquin. The majority of the invading army were Etruscans led by Lars Porsena of Clusium. The Etruscans approached Rome from the north and were met by the Roman army on the small plain by the Janiculum Hill. The Etruscans won the battle and surged forward, trying to get over the Sublicius Bridge and so enter Rome.

ABOVE At the Battle of Algidus the Roman commander Cincinnatus threw the Roman standard into enemy lines to encourage his men to attack to win it back

Three Roman officers - Spurius Lartius, Titus Herminius Aquilinus and Publius Horatius - ran to hold the bridge against the Etruscans. Men from Rome began hacking at the wooden supports to the bridge. Lartius and Herminius fell back, but Horatius held firm until the bridge had collapsed. He then swam over the Tiber to reach Rome. The act of Horatius meant Porsena and Tarquin had to lay siege to Rome rather than take it quickly. Porsena chose to make peace and Tarquin did not recover Rome.

In 474 Etruscan naval power was smashed by the navies of the Greek cities in southern Italy. This Battle of Cumae effectively halted Etruscan expansion to the south and relieved pressure on Rome, the northernmost of the Latin League cities.

The fertile plains of Latium were not, however, to be left in peace. The Appennine Mountains to the south and east were occupied by wild hill tribes, the Volsci and Aequi, who frequently raided the more settled farming communities of the Tiber Valley. In about 480 the Volscians launched a major raid, capturing the towns of Antium and Tarracina before they retreated, loaded down with booty.

In 460 the Aequi mounted a major effort, aimed directly at Rome. The Senate realised it faced a crisis and after a heated debate called on the famous general Lucius Qunitus Cincinnatus to become Dictator. This unusual office was a purely temporary position lasting just 6 months. The Senate and Consuls would between them appoint a Dictator only if Rome was in dire trouble and a strong central command was necessary. When a Dictator was appointed the Consuls and all other elected officials had to stand down, the new leader being able to appoint whoever he chose to fill government positions. During his months in office, the Dictator was able to make or abolish laws, inflict punishments and spend money entirely as he saw fit. The only limit set to the Dictator's power was that he had to stand down after six months.

Cincinnatus was enjoying his retirement on his farm when he received his appointment to absolute power. He left his plough where it was, rode off to command the army and defeated the Aequi in a lightning campaign. He then resigned his power and returned to his farm to continue ploughing where he had left off just 16 days earlier. This ac-

LEFT At first Rome did not have a fleet, but as its territories grew the Romans began to build both merchant and war ships at the mouth of the Tiber River

RIGHT The Etruscan city of Veii was captured by a stratagum when Roman soldiers entered caves under the city and tunnelled upwards to get inside the city walls

tion of Cincinnatus was to be held up by later generations as an example to successful generals ambitious for political power, but was generally disregarded.

The fighting against the hill tribes flared into a full scale war in the 430s in which the Latins at first came off worst. The turning point came at the Battle of Algidus in 431. According to later accounts, the Aequi had driven back the first two ranks of the legions, the hastati and principes, and were pushing hard on the triari reserves. A Roman officer then hurled the legion standard into the ranks of the enemy. Thinking their sacred standard was being carried off as a trophy of war, the Romans surged forward to recover it and broke the enemy formation. Although the Volsci and Aequi had been defeated, it took another ten years of campaigning by the Latin League before they were overcome completely and forced into a peace treaty.

In 406 the Romans felt strong enough to move against the Etruscans. Their first target was the city of Veii, just four hours march north of Rome. This heavily fortified city stood on an isolated limestone hill, the steep slopes of which were topped by formidable stone walls. These stone walls were even more impregnable than they appeared. While the walls of other cities were about seven feet thick, those of Veii were terraced into the steep slopes of the hill on which they stood. Effectively the rear of the walls was filled by solid rock and rammed earth, so that the land behind the parapet was level, but that in front fell sheer for 30 feet or more. Stones hurled by siege engines made little impression on the walls, the force of the blow being simply absorbed.

Each summer for nine years the Roman army marched on Veii, and each year it was forced to retreat as the campaigning season ended. Eventually, in 396 BC, the Roman army attacking Veii was put under the command of Marcus Furius Camillus.

Camillus' first move was to persuade the Roman Senate to pay wages to those citizens willing to serve full time at the siege. This gave Camillus a permanent force to train in siege warfare, rather than a succession of militia units. Camillus then sent a team of military engineers into the drains under Veii. The engineers reported back that the drains had been blocked with stone rubble near where they would emerge into the city. Camillus reasoned that the entrances to these tunnels inside Veii would be guarded against a Roman force breaking through, so ordered his engineers to use the drains to get close to the city, then dig new tunnels up to the surface. This they did, emerging into a temple as a priest was completing a sacrifice. Roman soldiers poured through the tunnel and Veii fell.

This was the first time the Romans had successfully completed a siege of a fortified city. Camillus was awarded the honour of holding a Triumph in Rome, a military procession through the streets followed by sacred rituals.

The capture of the city of Veii was celebrated in Rome as an important victory over the Etruscan confederation of cities which had for many years threatened Rome from the north. In truth the victory had been won principally because the bulk of the Etruscan armies were busy in the north fighting against a wave of barbaric Celtic tribes pouring over the Alps from central Europe.

The Celts represented something entirely new to warfare in Italy. The northerners were tall and broad, on average a good 6 inches taller than the Romans, and their fair hair and pale skins made them even stranger in appearance. The

ABOVE A Roman army fights a force of Celtic warriors. The tall, powerful Celts struck fear into the Romans, but eventually better discipline gave victory to Rome

Celts wore bright clothes, painted their shields with dramatic patterns and had towering plumes of feathers and horsehair on their helmets. They sang, chanted, blew trumpets and screamed abuse as they formed up to fight. They were, in short, a terrifying sight when encountered in battle.

Most Celtic armies included substantial numbers of cavalry, the Celtic

love of horses and horsemanship being a constant feature of ancient accounts. These horsemen were used extensively for scouting and raiding, allowing a Celtic chieftain to have a good idea of the lands through which he was marching and to know if an enemy army was close to his own. In battle the cavalry were used as a mobile strik-ing force, though they lacked the shock power needed to break dense formations of infantry.

The Celts had begun moving over the Alps around 450 BC. The first tribes to arrive, the Insubres, Boii, Lingones and Cenomani, took over the rich farming lands of the Po Valley, driving out or enslaving the native inhabitants. Around 400 BC a new tribe, more numerous than the others arrived. These were the Senones, who came from southern Germany. The Senones passed through the lands of the settled tribes, picking up many warriors as they passed, then pushed into Etruscan territory in search of loot, plunder and land on which to settle. The Senones were led by a man the Romans call Brennus in their histories, though this is the Celtic title for a war leader rather than a personal name.

As Brennus and his Celts swept through Etruscan lands they defeated the army of Clusium, also killing a pair of Roman envoys who had been with the Etruscan force. The Romans, rashly, sent ambassadors to the Celtic King Brennus demanding compensation. Brennus's only response was to march his army towards Rome. At this crucial point, Rome's most successful general was in exile. Marcus Furius Camillus had been accused of helping himself to a large quantity of the plunder from the capture of Veii instead of passing it all to the Roman treasury. As a result Camillus was living at Ardea and was unavailable to face the Celts. His colleague as Consul, Lucius Lucretius, therefore had undivided command of the army, but little in the way of skill.

On 18th July 390 BC a Roman army of about 40,000 men drew up for battle astride the road from Clusium to Rome where it forded the small River Allia about 15 miles north of their home city. When Brennus and his army came into sight it was clear they outnumbered the Romans by about two to one. The Celts formed up into a long battle line, accompanied by their usual singing and chanting, then surged forwards. Unlike the Italian enemies the Romans were accustomed to facing, the Celts made no attempt to deploy into clever tactical formations but simply charged home with screaming and fanatical fury. The Roman army broke, to be slaughtered in their thousands by the jubilantly pursuing Celts.

The Battle of the Allia was over in minutes, but it was the worst defeat Rome had suffered. Now Rome itself lay almost unprotected before the advancing barbarians. The only military force in the city was a guard of older men under the command of Marcus Manlius, who had been a Consul some years earlier and was therefore considered fit for military command. Manlius hurriedly set about preparing the city for the coming attack.

The Roman troops fleeing before the victorious Celts at the Battle of the Allia headed in many directions, though most made for the impressive fortress of Veii, a few miles to the west. It took the Celtic leader Brennus some hours to gather together his victorious, but unruly warriors. By the time this was achieved it was nightfall so Brennus ordered his men to camp for the night and to advance on Rome the following morning.

When the Celtic army marched on Rome they found the city apparently deserted. The walls around the city were unmanned, the gates hanging open on their hinges. The Romans had made the most of their night's reprieve before the Celts arrived. Marcus

Manlius had decided on a dramatic defence strategy. As an experienced commander, Manlius knew that the few men he had in the city would be unable to defend the entire perimeter wall, so he abandoned most of the city and planned to hold only the steep and well defended Capitol Hill. To keep his needs for food and water to a minimum, Manlius decided that only fit young fighting men would remain in Rome. The women and children were sent off before dawn to head for the fortifications of the city of Caere, taking with them all the moveable wealth that could be carried.

The Celts entered Rome in the morning and wandered through the streets, breaking into houses and temples to take whatever they fancied. When they reached the Forum the Celts found some of the oldest Roman Senators seated on their ivory chairs and dressed in their togas of rank. It is not clear if the old men were expecting to negotiate a truce, or were simply too frail to march to Caere. Unable to talk Latin, the Celtic warriors milled around the Senators waiting for Brennus to arrive. One Celt reached out to touch one of the Romans, a senator named Marcus Papirius, but had his hand struck away by the old

Roman. The Celt promptly killed the man and his companions. Any chance of parley or truce was over.

The Roman soldiers barricaded into the fortifications on top of the Capitol Hill watched the events in the Forum grimly. They were too few in number to intervene and, in any case, their main task to was hold the Capitol on which were stored the statues of the gods and the main wealth of Rome. Lacking any siege equipment, the Celts could not break in and instead settled down to starve the Romans out. It proved to be a long task and the Celts were eager to leave the empty city for new areas to plunder.

Brennus noticed that one section of the Capitol was protected by a sheer cliff, but that on top of the rock face was a temple of Juno, not fortifications. He sent for those men who were skilled at rock climbing and ordered them to scale the cliff after dark. Brennus hoped that these men would then form a defensive ring while they let down rope ladders up which more warriors could climb. He knew that if he could get enough men on to the Capitol he would be able to overwhelm the few defenders. At first everything went well for the Celts as they reached the foot of the cliff unobserved and began to climb. When the first Celt reached the top of his climb, however, he disturbed a cage of sacred geese kept in the temple of Juno. The birds set up a loud and persistent squawking which brought Marcus Manlius and his Roman soldiers running to the spot in time to push the Celts back.

After seven months of stalemate, the invaders were as keen to return home as the defenders were to be rid of them. The Romans agreed to pay the Celts several pounds weight of gold to make peace. As the gold was being weighed out the Romans noticed that the weights supplied by the Celts were heavier than those agreed, meaning the Romans were paying more gold than they expected. The Romans objected, but Brennus simply pulled out his sword and dropped it on top of the fraudulent weights. He glared at the Romans and declared "Woe to the conquered". The surrounding Celt warriors fingered their own swords menacingly. The Romans paid up.

The Celtic occupation of Rome left deep scars on the Roman mind. Never again would the Romans leave their city undefended. Faced by a potential

LEFT The Celts failed to capture the Capitoline Hill. When they attempted to scale the walls the sacred geese in the Temple of Juno began cackling and alerted the Roman defenders

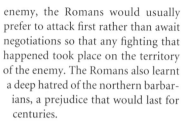

enemy, the Romans would usually prefer to attack first rather than await negotiations so that any fighting that happened took place on the territory of the enemy. The Romans also learnt a deep hatred of the northern barbarians, a prejudice that would last for centuries.

Having rid themselves of the Celts, the Romans were faced with a home city burned to the ground, Latin allies who now looked on Rome as a defeated power and surrounding states eager to take advantage of the Latin weakness. To solve these problems, the Romans turned to Lucius Furius Camillus, the general who had captured Veii.

Camillus was appointed to be the Dictator of Rome. Camillus devoted his

powers as Dictator to the army. Having chased the few marauding bands of looting Celts out of Latium, Camillus returned to Rome and sacked every military official, reappointing only those he trusted. He then reformed the Roman army to become a more effective instrument of war. Later Roman writers gave the credit for many military innovations to Camillus, even those that occurred a generation earlier or later. It is certain, however, that it was Camillus who introduced new pieces of equipment to the Roman army that were copied from the Celts.

With this newly re-equipped army, Rome quickly re-established itself as the dominant city of the Latin League. In 360 BC the Celts returned, pouring down the east coast of Italy, then crossing the mountains to fall on the rich plains of Latium. The Latins fell back into their fortified cities rather than face the Celts in open battle. Finding little to eat and no plunder worth taking, the Celts retreated. Ten years later they invaded again. This time the Romans led a Latin army out to face the invaders. As the armies drew up for battle, a gigantic Celt stepped forward and challenged any Roman who dared to a single combat.

**FAR LEFT** A Celtic warrior of about 400 BC. He carries a large oblong wooden shield and wears a bronze helmet topped by a decorative crest. His sword and spear are both made of iron

**LEFT** At the Battle of the Allia the Romans were heavily defeated by a force of Celts and all of central Italy was left open to Celtic plundering

nickname Corvus, meaning 'crow', and went on to lead his men to victory over the Celts.

Meanwhile, the Etruscans had become seriously worried by the growing power of the Latin League of cities, led by Rome. In 356 BC the central and southern Etruscan cities banded together to attack Latium, but despite some savage battles the Etruscans failed to make any real impression on their enemy. In 351 BC Rome and her allies captured the Etruscan city of Falerii, crushing the combined Etruscan armies in the field to do so. Rome now disbanded the Latin League and instead made individual treaties with each of the Latin cities, binding each of them firmly to Rome rather than to each other. Rome was now the dominant power in central Italy. To the north the remaining Etruscan cities were becoming subservient to the Celtic tribes settling in the Po Valley. To the south the civilised Greek cities were gradually succumbing to another rising power, the Samnites.

ABOVE A plaque made in Italy in about 1550 shows Horatius at the bridge

RIGHT A map of Italy in about 350 BC showing the main peoples and areas

The challenge was taken up by Marcus Valerius. As the two men fought a crow flew down and pecked at the Celt's face, distracting him enough to allow Valerius to kill him. Valerius then took the

RIGHT A German engraving made in 1586 by artist Hendrick Goltzius shows Horatius with, in the background, his famous fight at the bridge

By 340 BC the boundary between the growing empire of Rome and the southern territory dominated by the Samnites, from the city of Samnium, was fixed on the Liris River. Before long border skirmishes broke out and both sides accused the other of violating the agreed frontier. Known to later historians as the First Samnite War, this low key conflict soon fizzled out.

Small scale though the fighting against the Samnites had been, it had been enough to convince the Romans that they had a tough new enemy to contend with. Still smarting from the Celtic sack of Rome itself, the Romans were determined to take the initiative against the Samnites rather than wait to see what diplomacy or friendship could achieve. In 328 BC they planted a colony at Fregallae, on the south bank of the Liris. The Samnites retaliated by ousting the pro-Roman government of Naples. Rome declared war.

The first years of war were spent in desultory skirmishing and diplomatic efforts to involve the cities of southern Italy on one side or the other. The indecisive nature of these years is partly explained by the very different fighting styles of the Romans and the Samnites.

The Romans fielded an army of heavy infantry, with cavalry and light infantry in secondary roles. The Samnites in contrast had their main strength in lightly armoured, agile infantry and cavalry. Although the Samnites could field armies of heavy infantry drawn from their Greek allies, they preferred not to rely on such troops as they could never really trust the notoriously fractious politics of the Greek cities. At any moment a city might decide to join the Romans, declare neutrality or fall to internal bickering that made its army useless in the field. Effectively the Samnites could move swiftly and easily through the mountains, while the Romans were invincible on the plains.

In 321 BC the Samnites launched a feint into the rich farming land of Apulia. Thinking that, at long last, the Samnites had committed their main force to the open plains, the Roman Consul Tiberius Veturius Calvinus massed the Roman army and set off in pursuit. To reach Apulia, Calvinus had to negotiate a mountain pass known as the Caudine Forks, from the city of Caudium nearby. The road first passed through a narrow defile, then across a wide but enclosed valley before climbing to pass through

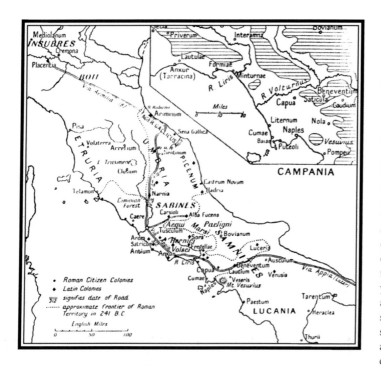

ABOVE A map of central Italy in about 250 BC showing the principal peoples, areas and cities

Faced by the seasoned mountain fighters, Calvinus was trapped. After a few futile attempts to force his way through the mountain passes, Calvinus realised his army was doomed to a slow starvation unless he sued for peace. Caius Pontius, the Samnite leader, was in no mood to be generous. He forced the Consul to agree to abandon all Rome's colonies and allies south of the Liris and to leave 600 of Rome's cavalry, the richest and noblest young men in the city, as hostages. Finally every single Roman soldier was stripped of arms, armour and even his clothing except for a shirt.

a second gorge. Calvinus marched through the first gorge without incident, but after crossing the plain found the second blocked by a large force of Samnites. Turning back, Calvinus was horrified the find the pass behind him blocked by a second force of the enemy.

The Romans were then forced to crawl under Samnite spears held barely two feet above the ground, while the watching Samnites jeered and insulted them. This was a well-established ritual humiliation known as 'passing under the yoke', but was usually inflicted on individuals as part of a legal punishment. To force an entire army to pass under the yoke was an unprecedented victory for the Samnites.

When the half-naked army walked barefoot into Rome the angry Senate had Calvinus thrown into prison. The Senate refused to ratify the treaty signed by Calvinus, but with most of their army disarmed there was little they could do to avenge the humiliation. The Caudine Peace, as it was known, looked set to endure.

Rome turned north to impose treaties favourable to itself on the Etruscan states still weak from fighting the Celts. Then the Aequi, Abruzzi and Vestini were defeated and their lands absorbed into the growing state of Rome. When the Samnites tried to annex the little town of Lucania in 298 BC the Romans felt strong enough to resist them.

The Samnites moved with their usual swiftness, sending a large army racing north through the Appennine Mountains to Sentinum, where it halted. The Samnites had been busy during the years of peace and had made alliances with Rome's enemies to the north, the Etruscans and the Celts. The Celts arrived quickly, but the Etruscan armies were still absent when the Romans were seen advancing.

The Romans had mustered their entire army, and those of their allies, for the campaign. The combined force was led by the two Consuls for the year, Quintus Fabius and Publius Decius Mus. As the two sides were deploying for battle Decius marched out in front of the Roman army accompanied by a group of priests. Performing sacrifices, Decius pledged his life and soul to the Gods before throwing off his armour and dressing as a priest. Thus arrayed, Decius drew a sword and raced at the Samnites, killing several in a frenzied outburst of violence before he was cut down. The battle that followed lasted many hours and ended in complete victory for Rome and her allies. Fabius led the army on a march through Etruscan territory compelling city after city to surrender and submit to a very unequal alliance with Rome.

In 293 BC, the Romans finally invaded the Samnite homeland itself. At the Battle of Aquilonia over 20,000 Samnites were killed and 97 military standards were captured. So many prisoners were taken that their sale in the slave markets raised 2.5 million pounds of bronze and 1,830 pounds of silver bullion for the Roman treasury. In

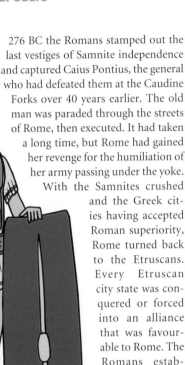

276 BC the Romans stamped out the last vestiges of Samnite independence and captured Caius Pontius, the general who had defeated them at the Caudine Forks over 40 years earlier. The old man was paraded through the streets of Rome, then executed. It had taken a long time, but Rome had gained her revenge for the humiliation of her army passing under the yoke.

With the Samnites crushed and the Greek cities having accepted Roman superiority, Rome turned back to the Etruscans. Every Etruscan city state was conquered or forced into an alliance that was favourable to Rome. The Romans established new colonies throughout Etruria, populating these new fortified towns with Latins that could be trusted. All of Italy south of the Po Valley had been conquered by Rome. The city seemed supreme and the Roman government settled down to enjoy the fruits of conquest. They were in for a rude shock.

The city which resented Roman interference most was Taranto, then a prosperous business centre which drew its wealth from the large harbour and the trade which passed through it between Italy and the eastern Mediterranean. In 282 BC a fleet of ten Roman warships appeared off Taranto and rowed straight into the harbour. The treaty between Taranto and Rome had specifically stated that no warships were to enter the harbour without permission. The Taranto government saw this action as one arrogant flouting of the treaty too many. The Roman fleet was attacked, four ships being sunk and the admiral drowned.

Rome sent a group of senators led by Lucius Postumius to Taranto to demand an apology and compensation. The Tarentines were not interested and when Postumius stood to address them, they laughed at his poor Greek and threw food and dirt at him. As Postumius left he was grabbed from behind by a drunken actor. Turning angrily, Postumius pushed the

FAR LEFT A Samnite warrior. His armour is of bronze and was famously high quality. The coloured feathers on his helmet may have indicated his rank

LEFT In 282 BC the Roman ambassador to Taranto, Lucius Postumius, was ridiculed and taunted when he tried to make a speech, an act that led to war

man aside then held up his stained toga. "You can laugh now," he declared. "But I will wash my clothes clean in rivers of your blood." War was inevitable.

Rome mustered an army of 25,000 men and sent it south, confident that they could quickly capture Taranto. In fact, the Tarentines were equally confident of victory having already gained the support of Pyrrhus, King of Epirus. Related to Alexander the Great, Pyrrhus was one of the greatest soldiers in the Greek world. He had served under several of Alexander's generals and, by 280 BC when he arrived in Taranto, had trained and equipped the Epirot army to the highest standards, fighting in the style of Alexander the Great.

The army Pyrrhus brought to Italy was made up of 20,000 heavy infantry, 2,000 archers, 500 slingers, 3,000 cavalry and 20 war elephants. He could also count for support on the army of Taranto and, he hoped, other Greek cities in Italy. The core of Pyrrhus's army was the unit known as the syntagma, 256 heavy infantry drawn up in a solid mass, 16 men across the front and 16 men deep. Each individual syntagma could operate on its own, or join with others to create a more massive formation. Each man was equipped with a mail tunic, which reached to below the groin, a bronze helmet and a round bronze shield. The main offensive weapon was a steel-tipped pike about 23 feet long, though each man had a short sword as well.

In battle, the front five ranks held their pikes forward to form a solid mass of points facing the enemy, while the rear ranks held their pikes sloping forward to break the flight of incoming javelins and arrows. The syntagma could stand solidly in defence, or advance at a trot to build up enough momentum simply to roll over any infantry force in its path. Success depended largely on exact co-operation between the different ranks, which in turn was possible only after many months of intense training. The army of Pyrrhus was superbly trained, but losses could not be replaced by the militia armies of Taranto and her allies.

Pyrrhus met the advancing Roman army at Heraclea. The two masses of armoured infantry fought each other to a stalemate, but Pyrrhus used his elephants and cavalry with skill and drove the Romans back in confusion. Both sides spent the winter wooing the Greek cities of southern Italy, while Rome trained a fresh army. In 279 BC

LEFT At the Battle of Heraclea King Pyrrhus of Pontus defeated the Romans using his war elephants, but lost so many men that he decided to make peace

Pyrrhus faced a Roman army 40,000 strong at Asculum. Battle was joined in wooded country where the inflexible Epirot syntagma was at a disadvantage against the more mobile Roman legion. The fighting raged all day long. On the second day, Pyrrhus lured the Romans on to a plain and again defeated them with his cavalry and elephants. It had been a bruising encounter, however. Pyrrhus had lost 4,000 of his trained men. "One more victory like that," he remarked, "and we are finished." The phrase Pyrrhic Victory has come to mean a victory gained at such a heavy cost that it is more like a defeat.

The war dragged on for another four years with neither side willing to risk a major battle. A conflict at Beneventum in 275 BC saw more losses for Pyrrhus. Soon afterwards, news came from Epirus of an unexpected invasion by the Macedonians. Pyrrhus took the remnants of his army, barely 10,000 men, back home. He left a garrison in Taranto and promised to return as soon as he had defeated Macedonia. In the event Pyrrhus never returned to Italy. In 272 BC Taranto made peace with Rome. The Epirot garrison was replaced with a Roman one and Taranto forced to send its most important citizens to live in Rome as hostages.

The wars against Pyrrhus showed that the Roman legions could take on the best soldiers in the known world. Although Pyrrhus had won the battles, Rome had won the war. There was no doubt that Rome was ruler of Italy, and her military reputation was the highest in the western Mediterranean.

But winning wars was not the only route to wealth in the ancient world, there was

LITTLE BOOK OF **ANCIENT ROME**

another - trade. The main trade routes of the western Mediterranean were controlled by a city every bit as wealthy and impressive as Rome, the city of Carthage in North Africa.

Carthage had been founded as a colony by Phoenician sailors from what is now Lebanon about 80 years before Rome was founded by Romulus. While Rome had fought her wars with Celts, Samnites, Etruscans and Epirots, Carthage had built a huge navy of war and merchant ships with which to dominate the trade routes. Almost every port in North Africa outside Egypt and western Sicily was under Carthaginian control. Although Carthage had a powerful navy, her army was small and weak, so the city hired large numbers of mercenaries to make up numbers.

For many years, Rome had been at peace with Carthage. The two cities agreed a series of trade treaties and exchanged regular diplomatic missions. During the war with Pyrrhus, Carthage had sent her fleet to help Rome. But during the years after the defeat of Pyrrhus tension between the two powers increased. In 264 BC the largest Greek city on Sicily, Syracuse, was at war with Carthage and her ally the city of Messina, which controlled the narrow straits between Sicily and Italy. Syracuse was on the point of capturing Messina when a strong Carthaginian force arrived, drove them out and took up residence in the city. The Messinians may have been allies of Carthage, but had no wish to have a force of foreign soldiers stationed amongst them. They appealed to Rome for help in ousting the garrison.

Rome did not want the powerful Carthaginian navy to have a base so close to Italy and had much preferred the situation when eastern Sicily was divided between squabbling Greek city states. Although intervention would involve war with both Carthage and Syracuse, Rome sent a small fleet to Messina. The Carthaginian fleet offshore thought they were at peace with Rome and hesitatingly let the Romans through. The Carthaginian garrison was ousted and the newly combined army of Messina and Rome marched on Syracuse. The First Punic War had begun. The Romans referred to Carthage as Punicus, so the wars against that city were called the Punic Wars.

For four years the Roman army made steady progress in Sicily, capturing towns and penning the Carthaginian forces into the western end of the island. Ultimate victory was, however, prevented by the

LEFT After the sacking of Rome by the Celts in 390 BC large areas of the city remained in ruins for years until a determined effort to rebuild and repopulate the city were made

Carthaginian fleet which kept the Roman force in Sicily short of supplies and men. In 260 BC the Romans built a fleet of 120 ships and sent it out under the command of the Consul Cornelius Duillius.

The Romans claimed that they copied the design of a Carthaginian ship which ran aground on the Italian coast, but it is at least as likely that they employed the skilled shipwrights of their allies in the Greek cities of southern Italy. The Roman ships were similar to those of Carthage in being long, narrow vessels powered chiefly by dozens of oarsmen arranged in three banks along either side. The key difference lay in the way in which the ships were used in fighting. The Carthaginians relied on the speed and discipline of their oarsmen to outmanoeuvre an enemy ship and ram it, causing it to sink or be crippled. The Romans packed their ships with soldiers and relied on boarding to win a battle. The soldiers boarded the enemy ship by means of a pivoting gangway equipped with a spike to secure it to the opposing vessel. This corvus, or 'crow', was a new invention and it took the Carthaginians by surprise.

The first naval clash came in the waters off Mylae and ended with a crushing Roman victory. The corvus had proved its worth. Two years later the Romans won a second naval battle and now it was the Carthaginians on Sicily who were running short of supplies. Encouraged by success the Romans used their fleet to transport a large army under the Consul C. Attilius Regulus to Africa to attack Carthage itself. The Carthaginians responded by hiring a band of Greek mercenaries led by the Spartan Xanthippus, who promptly wiped out the entire Roman force. The same year the Romans lost a fleet of 350 ships to a vicious storm.

In Sicily the new Carthaginian commander, Hamilcar Barca, began an inspired campaign of guerrilla warfare that saw him raid the Italian mainland itself and gradually grind down the Roman forces in Sicily. The Carthaginian government had, however, lost interest in the war. They were exploring exciting new trading opportunities in Spain and Gaul and were not willing to spend the money on an expensive war with Rome. Carthage gave Sicily to Rome as the price of peace and called Hamilcar Barca home.

The furious Hamilcar took his young son to the Temple of Baal in Carthage and together the father and son swore an oath of undying hatred against Rome. The boy's name was Hannibal.

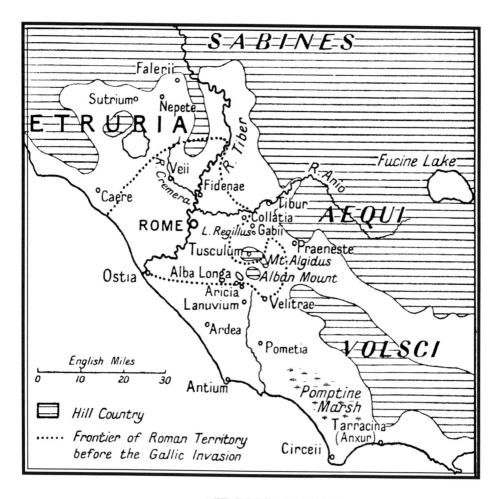

# Political Jobs in the Roman Republic

## Consul

Two consuls were elected each year. They headed up the government of Rome and chaired meetings of the Senate. They had the right to command the army in important campaigns. Until 367 BC only patricians could be elected consul, after that year one had to be plebeian and one either a patrician or an equite. Only men aged over 40 who had already served as a quaestor and a praetor could stand for election. Having served as consul it was illegal to stand for election again for at least 10 years, though this rule was sometimes ignored.

## Praetor

The first Praetor was elected in 367 BC. In 246bc a second was added and then four more in 197bc. Praetors were in charge of the administration of justice, organizing sittings of the law courts and ensuring that the law was adhered to. A Praetor could also be sent by a Consul to do any job that the Consul was too busy to do himself. Until 337 BC only Patricians could be elected to be Praetor, but after that date any citizen could stand for election. After 227 BC special additional Praetors could be elected for a one year term to perform some special task. The decision whether or not to have an additional Praetor was made by the Senate.

## Censors

The two censors were elected every five years. These officials drew up the lists of who was a Roman citizen and decided to which social class they belonged. The censors could remove citizenship or downgrade a person's social status for immoral behaviour and so came to have great social power. They took a very dim view of citizens working in certain jobs - such as acting in theatres - of citizens who beat their children or slaves excessively, of citizens who did not get married and a host of other immoral acts that changed over time. Often the mere threat of a visit from the censors would cause a Roman citizen to change his behaviour.

## Aediles

There were four aediles elected each year. They were in charge of maintaining public buildings - such as roads, defensive walls, aqueducts and drains - and of organizing festivals and public events. An aedile had to be at least 27 years old and had to have already been a Quaestor.

## Quaestors

Until 267 BC four quaestors were elected each year, after that date there were ten. Quaestors were financial officials who supervised tax collection, made sure public money was spent properly and inspected all public accounts for signs of bribery, theft or other improper actions. After having served as a Quaestor a man could sit and vote in the Senate and was given the title "senator".

## Tribunes

The number of tribunes varied over time. Any adult plebeian could stand for election to be a tribune, and only plebeians could vote in the election. A tribune had no specific duties of his own, but could question any of the other officials about what they were doing and issue a "veto" or an instruction telling an official to stop a particular action. Anyone who laid hands on a tribune, and any official who refused a direct instruction from a tribune, was punished by public execution.

## Promagistrate

This was a temporary office that allowed the Senate to appoint a man to take over the duties of an official who had died or was too ill to do his job properly. A person appointed in this way had to have already been elected to the position in a previous year and held office only until the next election was due. Some times a man would be appointed as a promagsitrate to be an additional official in order to carry out a specific task.

## Governor

A governor was an official sent away from Rome to do a task on behalf of the Senate. At first these tasks could be almost anything, but gradually a governor came to be a man put in charge of ruling a province that belonged to Rome. He would be in charge of all aspects of government in the province, including the legal system, tax collection and commanding troops.

# Chapter 3

# THE GREAT REPUBLIC

**Having won the war with Carthage, and gained control of the productive farmlands of Sicily, Rome was suddenly thrown on to the defensive by two fresh enemies.**

The war with the Celts began due to the Celtic resentment of the Roman colonies established at Rimini and Spezia and started with a Celtic attack designed to contain Roman power south of the Arno River. In 225 BC the Celtic army was defeated at the Battle of Telamon and in 221 BC their leaders made peace. The Roman victory was due to the steady discipline of the legions, compared to the flamboyant courage of the Celts.

The second war took Rome into entirely new territory. The east coast of the Adriatic Sea, an area known as Illyricum, had become united under an aggressive and imaginative queen named Teuta. Teuta first captured the Greek island of Corfu, putting it under her commander Demetrius, then loosed her ships to prey on the merchants of the area. In 230 BC these pirates attacked a flotilla of merchant ships from southern Italy. When Rome sent ambassadors to Teuta to protest, they were in turn attacked. In the war that followed Rome persuaded Demetrius to hand over Corfu and then went on to drive Teuta out of southern Illyricum before imposing a peace treaty that stripped her of her ships.

Carthage had, meanwhile, been rebuilding her merchant empire across North Africa and into Spain. As well

as extensive trading contacts across western Europe and along the Atlantic seaboard, Carthage conquered or made alliances with tribes and cities in mainland Spain itself. In 227 BC Carthage agreed with the Greek city of Marseille, an ally of Rome, that the River Ebro would be the boundary between their spheres of influence. In 221 BC a new commander took over the Carthaginian forces in Spain, Hannibal the son of Hamilcar Barca.

In 219 BC Hannibal occupied the city of Saguntum, ousting a government friendly to Marseille and Rome. The city was well south of the Ebro, so Hannibal felt he had a right to make the move. The Romans sent an envoy to Carthage in protest and, after some weeks of fruitless diplomacy, declared war.

Hannibal had, in fact, been preparing for war with Rome ever since taking command. His opening moves had been to ensure the loyalty of the allies and conquered areas of Spain. This was achieved by agreeing lucrative trade contracts and lenient treaties of alliance with those who could be won over and placing Carthaginian garrisons in the territories of those who could not. Hannibal put his brother Hasdrubal, in overall command of these garrisons.

Hannibal's next move was to make contact with the Celtic tribes of the Po Valley, so recently defeated by Rome. The reaction of the Celts was mixed. A few leaders were eager to have another war with Rome to win back lost territory, but most were wary of risking a second defeat and refused to support the Carthaginian openly.

Finally, Hannibal massed together an army for a daring invasion of Italy by way of the Pyrenees and the Alps. This army was a large one. At its core was a force of professional troops from Carthage and North Africa. Hannibal had about 20,000 such infantry, 6,000 cavalry and around 30 elephants. He also had another 6,000 cavalry and 70,000 infantry raised in Spain. In the spring of 218 BC, Hannibal marched north across the Ebro. The journey to Italy took almost the entire summer, but

**FAR LEFT** A Spanish soldier serving in the army of the great Carthaginian commander Hannibal. He has much lighter armour than a Roman soldier and carries javelins to hurl at the enemy

**LEFT** Hannibal recoils in horror as he sees the head of his beloved brother Hasdrubal which had been sent to him by the Romans to show they had crushed the reinforcements Hannibal was expecting

ABOVE The Roman
Empire in about 220 BC

RIGHT A bust of
Hannibal carved a few
years after his death

in the autumn of 218 BC he led his army
down from the Alps into the Po Valley
to receive a muted response from the
Celts he had hoped would be allies. They
told him bluntly that he needed to show
that he could defeat Rome before they
would join him. Hannibal promptly
lured a Roman force into attacking
across a boggy river at Trebia and massacred 20,000 Romans. The Celts rose in

rebellion against Rome.

The following spring Hannibal led
his mixed army of Carthaginians, North
African mercenaries, Spanish allies
and Celtic tribesmen south towards
the Arno Valley. Learning that a large
Roman army was advancing to meet
him, Hannibal turned eastwards as if
retreating in panic. The Consul in command of the pursuing Roman army,

Caius Flaminius, was determined to catch Hannibal and advanced at full speed.

As a misty dawn broke Flaminius was marching hard along the north shore of Lake Trasimeno with hills to his left and what appeared to be the retreating rearguard of Hannibal's army scampering away to his front. Suddenly thousands of Celts and Spanish infantry burst from cover in the hills and poured down on the Roman flank as the legions were strung out along the narrow road. The Romans found the road in front and behind blocked by solid masses of African armoured infantry. The fighting raged for three hours, but gradually the Romans were driven into the waters of the lake where their armour dragged them down to their deaths. About 3,000 Romans in the very front of their column managed to escape, but at least 15,000 were killed and another 15,000 surrendered. Flaminius himself was killed, though his body was never found. Hannibal had lost only 1,500 men.

ABOVE The wild
tribesmen of Thrace put
up a fierce resistance
to Rome, but were
eventually conquered
and remained part of
the Roman Empire for
600 years

The Second Punic War had begun badly for Rome. Worse was to come.

When the news of the defeat at Lake Trasimeno reached Rome, the Senate summoned all male citizens to the Forum to announce the bad news. Three days later they had to summon another meeting to announce that a second Roman army had been attacked by the Carthaginians and escaped only after suffering heavy losses.

While Hannibal marched on south towards Apulia in the hope of raising the Greek cities against Rome, the Roman senate debated what to do next. They chose to appoint as dictator a 60 year old veteran of the First Punic War named Quintus Fabius Maximus. The first action of Fabius was to raise a new army, recruiting four entirely new legions as well as bringing up to strength those already defeated by Hannibal.

Fabius then set out with a force of around 50,000 men to track Hannibal south. Fabius did not intend to fight a battle but instead to follow what became

LITTLE BOOK OF **ANCIENT ROME**

known as Fabian tactics, that is to say he attacked any foraging parties Hannibal sent out, blocked mountain passes and generally made life difficult for the enemy without risking a battle. The Fabian tactics hampered Hannibal's campaign, but the Roman Senate wanted victory. When Fabius's six months were up the huge new army he had raised was put under the command of the two newly elected Consuls, Gaius Terentius Varro and Lucius Aemilius Paulus. To avoid disputes the Consuls agreed to command the army on alternate days.

The Consuls marched south with an army of eight full-strength legions, about 80,000 men, plus 6,000 cavalry and a variety of lightly armed scouts and skirmishers. They caught up with Hannibal near the town of Cannae and established a camp fortified by ditches and wooden palisades. After several days of skirmishing, Varro thought he had found the ideal place on which to face Hannibal. On a day when he commanded the army, Varro marched out of

ABOVE Hannibal's capture of Saguntum after an 8 month siege started the Second Punic War between Rome and Carthage

camp to take up a position on the south bank of the River Ofanto. The right flank rested on the river while the left flank was protected by a range of low, steep hills.

From here Varro could stop the Carthaginians collecting forage and water. At the same time the narrow field meant that Hannibal could not take advantage of the superior speed and mobility of his lightly armed troops. Unlike in earlier encounters, Varro believed, the advantage would be with the heavy Roman legionaries. He left about 7,000 of the older men to guard his own camp and ordered them to attack Hannibal's camp if the opportunity arose.

While the Romans were still deploying, Hannibal marched out of his camp to take up the challenge. Hannibal placed his Spanish and Celtic infantry in the centre to face the Roman legionaries. His Numidian cavalry were on his right to face the cavalry of Rome's allies and his Spanish and Celtic cavalry on the left to face those of Rome. The crack Carthaginian heavy infantry were placed in two columns on either side of his centre.

Varro opened the battle by ordering his legions forward to the attack. As the legions advanced they pushed the Celts and Spanish back, but found the Carthaginian infantry held firm. The Roman legions were slowly advancing into a bulge in the enemy centre. At this point Paulus was injured by a heavy sling stone and knocked unconscious. Hannibal then ordered his left wing cavalry to attack. They outnumbered the Roman cavalry facing them by four to one and quickly defeated them back. While one force of horsemen drove the Romans from the field, a second wheeled round to the right to attack Varro's cavalry from the rear, just as the Numidians charged their front. Soon the second force of mounted Romans was in flight.

By now the legions were deep into the Carthaginian centre, though they had failed to break through as they expected. Suddenly they were attacked in the rear by the newly reformed enemy cavalry. Hannibal chose this moment to march his elite heavy infantry columns forward, face them inward and crush in the flanks of the legions. As the jaws of Hannibal's trap closed one Roman legion managed to fight its way out, just over 3,000 men escaped into the nearby hills. For the rest there was no escape. They could not run and, being increasingly squeezed between the converging enemy formations, they could not

deploy to fight. Around 60,000 Romans were butchered before Hannibal called an end to the killing, the final Roman death toll may have been as high as 70,000. No other single day of fighting has ever seen such a massive death toll. Even the trenches of the First World War fail to come close.

Rome appeared prostrate before the Carthaginian. But Rome was not in any mood to surrender.

When the terrible news from Cannae reached Rome the city panicked. A mob dragged out of the Temple of Vesta a Vestal Virgin who was suspected of breaking her vow of chastity and murdered her in the Forum. A Celtic couple in the city were pulled from their house and, in a

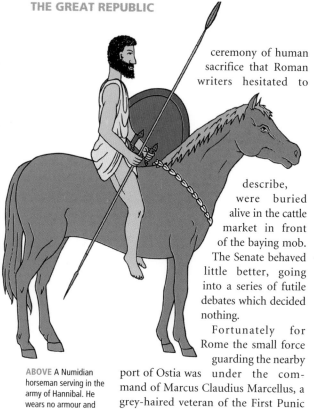

ceremony of human sacrifice that Roman writers hesitated to describe, were buried alive in the cattle market in front of the baying mob. The Senate behaved little better, going into a series of futile debates which decided nothing.

Fortunately for Rome the small force guarding the nearby port of Ostia was under the command of Marcus Claudius Marcellus, a grey-haired veteran of the First Punic War. He sent a force of marines to take over the walls of Rome, while marching his force to block the road from Cannae to Rome. Finding that Hannibal had continued south to raise the Samnites and Greeks against Rome, Marcellus

ABOVE A Numidian horseman serving in the army of Hannibal. He wears no armour and uses neither saddle nor stirrups

pushed on to link up with the 10,000 fugitives from Cannae. Likewise, Quintus Fabius Maximus moved quickly to install a Roman garrison in the citadel of Taranto and so stop Hannibal using that port to bring reinforcements from Africa or Spain. Naples was also reinforced, blocking that harbour to Carthaginian shipping.

During the months that followed Cannae, Hannibal marched around southern Italy rallying the opponents of Rome to his cause. Some cities joined the Carthaginians, others did not. The Romans, meanwhile, elected Marcellus and Fabius to be their Consuls and decided to continue the war until Hannibal had been driven out of Italy. The struggle dragged on for years. The Romans avoided battle, preferring the Fabian tactics to wear the enemy down. Without siege engines Hannibal could take neither Taranto nor Naples, let alone Rome, and so was cut off from supplies and reinforcements. Gradually Hannibal saw his forces weaken and his Italian allies overcome.

In 203 BC the Romans sent an army under the talented young general Publius Cornelius Scipio to invade Africa and attack Carthage. Hannibal

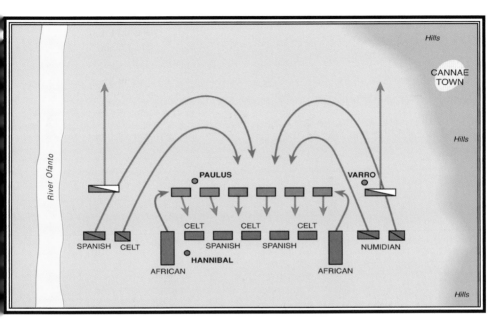

River Ofanto

Hills

CANNAE
TOWN

Hills

Hills

**PAULUS**

**VARRO**

CELT        CELT        CELT

SPANISH    SPANISH

SPANISH   CELT

NUMIDIAN

AFRICAN

**HANNIBAL**

AFRICAN

was recalled from Italy, slipping past a blockade of Roman ships with the remaining veterans at his disposal. Taking command of the Carthaginian army in Africa, Hannibal marched with around 28,000 men and 80 war elephants to face the 35,000 Romans.

Scipio had been a young officer at the battle of Lake Trasimeno and was among the cavalry who escaped from

Cannae. He had seen Hannibal at his best, and for years had been fighting the Carthaginian soldiers. He devised a plan to defeat the master. He drew up his legions in columns with maniples formed behind each other and lightly armed velites forming a skirmish line in front. For once the Romans had more cavalry than the Carthaginians, having persuaded a large number of Numidians

ABOVE The Battle of Cannae in 216 BC. Hannibal's Carthaginian army surrounded and then massacred the Roman army killing perhaps as many as 75,000 men

to join them in attacking Carthage.

The battle at Zama began with a prolonged period of skirmishing and cavalry feints before Hannibal sent in his elephants. These powerful, but cumbersome beasts, were lured by the velites between the Roman columns where they could be taken from behind and disabled, then killed. With the elephants dealt with, Scipio moved his infantry forwards. Unable to use his cavalry to outmanoeuvre the Romans, Hannibal tried to break the Roman centre with an advance of pikemen, but failed. Seeing the battle lost, Hannibal rode back to Carthage to organise a last ditch defence.

The Carthaginian government was not willing to fight to the death. They asked Scipio for peace terms. Scipio demanded Carthage abandon its lands in Spain and even most of its ports in Africa. Carthage agreed, but the Roman Senate was not satisfied with defeating Carthage. They wanted revenge on Hannibal and demanded that he be handed over. Carthage agreed, but Hannibal had fled.

For years Hannibal kept on the move. Whenever the Romans found where he was they sent ambassadors to threaten war unless he was handed over, but there was always time for the fugitive to move on. In 188 BC a Roman force finally cornered Hannibal in Bithynia. Seeing that he had no escape, Hannibal committed suicide remarking to his servant "Now let us put an end to the great anxiety of the Romans who have thought it too lengthy and too great a task to wait for the death of a hated old man."

While Rome had been embroiled in the life or death struggle with Carthage, she had inadvertently got involved in another and far more tortuous diplomatic and political struggle that would quickly lead to yet another war. Rome had become involved in Greece.

Roman lands in Illyricum had been taken by Macedonia so, after the Battle of Zama, Rome sent an army commanded by Titus Quinctius Flamininus across the Adriatic . The war against Philip V of Macedonia came to a head in 197 BC at the Battle of Cynoscephalae. Ever since the wars against Pyrrhus, Rome had been facing enemies whose armies had a core of heavily armoured pikemen which formed into dense formations 16 men deep known as the phalanx. Pyrrhus had used the formation to roll over the Romans, though at great cost. Hannibal preferred to use the

phalanx to deliver a crushing blow once the Romans were disordered by ambush or cavalry. At Cynoscephalae Flamininus showed that the Romans had finally found the answer to the phalanx.

The key to victory it seemed was to keep the maniples of legionaries on the move and not allow them to stand still to

be destroyed by the advancing phalanx. When Philip led his phalanx forwards, the Romans to their front simply fell back, allowing the Macedonians to tire and lose formation. Other Roman units, meanwhile, marched quickly around the flank to attack the Macedonians from the side. The phalanx was powerful, but unable to change direction easily once launched forwards. King Philip lost half his army dead, wounded or captured while the Romans lost fewer than 1,000 men.

Flamininus had been ordered merely to regain lost lands, so he did no more than impose a harsh peace on Macedon. One clause in the agreement was for Macedonian control over the cities of Greece to be removed. When this was announced at Corinth, Flamininus found himself hailed as a liberator of the Greeks and showered with honours.

Unfortunately for Greece, Rome was by now determined on building an empire. The men involved in public life were becoming increasingly corrupt and dishonest. Warfare against a civilised opponent was proving to be a profitable business both for Rome and for her armies as the loot from the conquered flowed into the home city. More particularly the generals gained both wealth and prestige, which furthered their political ambitions in Rome, allowing them to reach even higher and more lucrative positions in the Republic. It would not be long before the wealthy, but militarily weak cities of Greece proved too much of a temptation.

The first city to fall to the new Roman greed for conquest was her old enemy Carthage. In 150 BC Carthage objected to one of the more onerous provisions of the peace treaty which had been agreed after her defeat at Zama. Rome regarded this as an excuse for war and attacked. After a siege of three years Carthage fell amid scenes of savage street fighting. The entire population was sold into slavery, the city levelled and the surrounding fields ploughed with salt to destroy their fertility.

Meanwhile, in 149 BC, a man named Andriscus claimed to be the lawful heir of Philip V of Macedon and demanded the throne. An uprising threw out the clique of noblemen ruling the country on behalf of Rome and quickly led to the neighbouring territory of Thrace declaring war on Rome. In Greece, Corinth was emboldened to expel Roman envoys in disgrace.

Once Carthage had been destroyed, Rome turned on Macedon. An army under Quintus Caecilius Metellus crushed the forces of Andriscus and drove the Thracians back to their own country. Metellus proceeded to reorganise Macedon as a Roman province before advancing south on Greece. Metellus's period in office ended in this moment of victory and his place was taken by Lucius Mummius.

The new commander was the appointee of a faction in the Roman senate, but lacked any real talent or learning. When Corinth surrendered in 146bc Mummius imposed a savage peace. The city was at least a thousand years old and one of the most beautiful and cultured in Greece. Mummius did not care. He sold the entire population into slavery, stripped the city of every object that could be moved and burned what was left to the ground, demolishing the stone defensive walls. When drawing up a contract with the owner of a fleet of merchant ships to carry the priceless statues of Corinth back to Rome, Mummius included a clause that any works of art lost had to be replaced - ignoring the fact that some of the masterpieces were by artists long dead. Mummius did not care. Nor did Rome. The Roman state and army were embarked on a career of conquest.

LEFT A bust of Scipio Africanus, the general who defeated Hannibal, completed during his lifetime

Meanwhile social changes were taking place in Rome that were to have a profound effect. The great victories had led to a rise in wealth and power by the richer and more noble citizens as loot and prestige alike flooded into Rome. At the same time the huge number of slaves being dragged back to Roman territory undercut the wage of the poorer citizens, throwing them into unemployment and even greater poverty.

A politician named Tiberius Gracchus believed the answer to the growing problems lay in giving state-owned land to the poor plebeian citizens so that they could become small holders and farmers. This, Gracchus thought, would solve the unemployment issue and stabilise society. However the state lands he wanted to use were currently rented out, at low cost, to nobles and rich equite who used slaves to work the land and made huge profits. They stood to lose a vast income if Gracchus got his way. After years of tortuous political manoeuvring a gang of senators had Gracchus murdered in 133 BC.

Ten years later Tiberius's younger brother Gaius Gracchus tried again. Gaius decided that before seeking economic and land reform he should

first weaken the powers of the nobles in the Senate and other political offices that they held. Once again the political disputes followed many twists and turn, and once again the richer nobles turned to violence when it looked like they might lose. This time it was not only Gaius Gracchus who died, but some 3,000 of his supporters were butchered in a series of savage street battles.

The bloody careers of the Gracchi brothers did little to solve the underlying social and economic problems affecting Rome. What they did do was polarise Roman society into two factions. The optimates supported the rich noblemen and their grip on political, economic and social power. The populares favoured handing more power to the plebeians and giving poorer citizens more of a chance to rise socially and economically. Confusingly there were sometimes almost as many noblemen backing the populares as the optimates.

The second main outcome of the Gracchi disputes was that deadly violence was now seen as an option for solving political disputes.

The Roman armies that defeated Carthage, Macedon and Corinth were little changed in structure from that of three

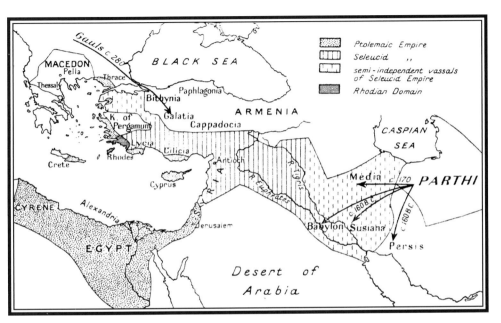

ABOVE A map of
the Near East in
about 180 BC

centuries earlier. But within scarcely more than a generation the Roman army would be transformed almost out of recognition. The changes were brought on by the enormous demands Rome was putting on her military. They would affect not only the army, but Rome itself.

While wars and campaigns were fought in Italy the citizens were asked to serve in the army for a few months in the summer every three or four years. Most were proud to serve the state in this way. By the mid-2nd century BC, however, Rome was fighting wars in Greece, Spain and North Africa. These campaigns kept men away from home for an entire year, sometimes more. Family men and those with businesses to look after resented these demands and recruitment became increasingly difficult.

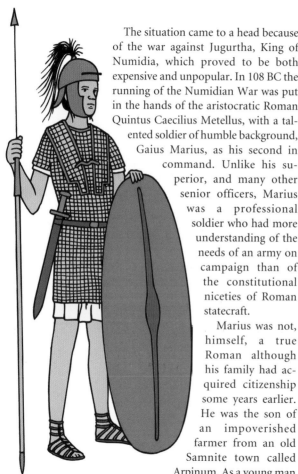

The situation came to a head because of the war against Jugurtha, King of Numidia, which proved to be both expensive and unpopular. In 108 BC the running of the Numidian War was put in the hands of the aristocratic Roman Quintus Caecilius Metellus, with a talented soldier of humble background, Gaius Marius, as his second in command. Unlike his superior, and many other senior officers, Marius was a professional soldier who had more understanding of the needs of an army on campaign than of the constitutional niceties of Roman statecraft.

Marius was not, himself, a true Roman although his family had acquired citizenship some years earlier. He was the son of an impoverished farmer from an old Samnite town called Arpinum. As a young man Marius scraped together enough money to purchase weapons and armour and so qualify for military service. Joining as a legionary, Marius rose quickly through the ranks thanks to his skill and dedication. He gathered enough money to qualify as an equite, the middle ranking of the Roman classes, and married into the well connected aristocratic Caesar family. After a few months in North Africa, Marius was so appalled by the mismanagement of the army that he decided to return to Rome and stand for election to the position of Consul. When he told his commanding officer of his plans, Metellus just laughed.

Nonetheless, Marius went to Rome and ran an election campaign based on the need to have a professional soldier in command of the army and promising to ensure that serving men had proper rations and equipment. He won a sweeping victory. In 107 BC the newly elected Consul Gaius Marius was put in charge of the war. His first move was to reform utterly the military system of Rome.

The changes brought in by Marius over the following years were to last for more than 400 years. They defined not just the role and performance of the army, but also the place of the army in

Roman society and government. In time the reforms of Marius came to affect the whole Roman world.

The most immediate problem facing Marius was recruitment. The well to do citizens who were eligible for enlistment simply did not want to serve overseas for long periods of time. Marius' solution was simple. He made every Roman citizen eligible for service in the army. Those who could not afford to supply their own weapons and equipment were provided with them by the state. This at once solved another problem that had long bedevilled professional soldiers like Marius, the fact that the legionaries turned up for service in and with a widely varied collection of armour and weaponry which differed as greatly in quality as it did in age and design.

To make service in the army even more attractive to the poorest citizens,

**LEFT** A Roman legionnary wearing the equipment laid down by Marius, including a coat of iron mail, large plywood shield and bronze helmet

**ABOVE** Marius reviews a legion equipped and trained in the new methods that he introduced to the Roman army

BELOW A marble
bust of Gaius Marius
completed a few years
after his death

Marius arranged for the soldiers to be paid while on service. Ever since the Siege of Veii over two centuries earlier, the Roman treasury had paid a few coins to serving men to help meet the expenses of campaign. Now Marius increased the pittance of expenses to become a living wage. The pay was graded according to rank. Suddenly service in the army ceased to be a duty owed to the state by its property-owning citizens. Instead it was a respectable career choice for the poor and destitute that offered good pay and the prospects of promotion and social advancement.

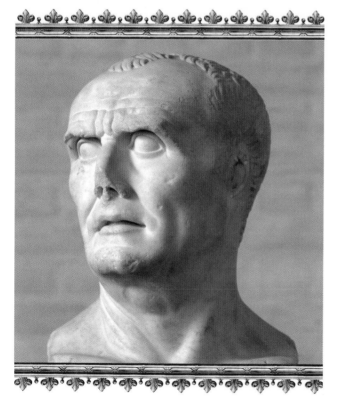

Marius gave Rome a professional army. No other state in the ancient world, except Sparta, had anything other than a militia strengthened by a professional command structure. This full time professional army gave important advantages to Rome. Not only could the army campaign at any time of year, when rival armies were denuded as men went home to gather in crops, but the men served for years on end and could be trained in complex manoeuvres and military engineering.

The years of Roman military supremacy were at hand, but so was her social collapse.

## Coins of the Rome

**Pecunia** - The first money used in Rome was an oblong ingot of copper stamped with a picture of a cow.

**Aes grave** - Used from about 300 BC this bronze coin carried the head of Janus on one side and a ship on the other.

**Semis** - Worth half an as this coin carried a picture of Jupiter on one side and a ship on the other.

**Dupondis** - Worth two as, the duponids had a picture of the goddess Roma on one side and a wheel on the other.

**Drachma** - First used in 281 BC silver coin copied from Greece that was used to pay soldiers, who were accustomed to getting one drachma a day. At first these showed the head of Mars on one side and a horse on the other, but later other designs were used.

**Dicrachm** - A silver coin worth two drachma.

**Denarius** - First produced in 211 BC the Denarius became the basis of Roman money. It was a silver coin worth 10 aes

**Sestersius** - Worth 2.5 aes, or a quarter of a denarius, the sestertius became the most common coin in Rome. Millions were produced with a wide variety of designs.

## Roman clothes

**Toga** - Worn by adult male citizens as smart or formal wear. The toga consisted of a single piece of wool or linen cloth 1.5 metres wide and 6 metres long. It was wrapped around the body then draped over the shoulder. By law the toga had to be worn by a citizen appearing in the Forum, in court or when voting.

**Stola** - A long, pleated dress worn by women that was fastened at the shoulders by two brooches and held in place by two belts, one just under the breasts and the second around the waist.

**Tunic** - Worn by men and women as an undergarment. This was shaped like a modern T-shirt but came down to about halfway between the waist and knees. The tunic might be worn on its own in hot weather.

**Palla** - An oblong-shaped shawl for women to wear over their heads and shoulders in bad weather.

**Pallium** - A long scarf worn around the neck and chest, sometimes wrapped over the head.

**Subligaculum** - A loin cloth worn srapped around the waist and looped between the legs.

# Chapter 4

# THE FALL OF THE REPUBLIC

For several decades after the death of Gaius Gracchus in 121bc the internal politics of Rome had been complex, vicious and often violent. The reforms of Marius had seemed at first to solve some of the problems by giving poorer citizens the option of a career in the army, and so eased the unemployment and poverty. In fact Marius had unwittingly provided a powerful new factor to Rome's troubles. The newly professionalised army gradually came to owe loyalty more to the generals and commanders than to the state.

This toxic mix of social problems, political violence and military power came to a head under the general and politician Sulla, more properly Lucius Cornelius Sulla.

Sulla had led a long and successful military career, and was a leading optimate, when in 84 BC crisis struck. The consul in Rome, Cinna, was murdered and chaos spread. Sulla was in Asia Minor (now Turkey) where he had been fighting a war. Now he gathered his army together and marched on Rome itself. Sulla declared that he was coming to restore order, but many feared he was coming to impose optimate power.

The newly elected consuls announced that Sulla must not bring armed men to Rome. When Sulla showed no signs of halting his march they raised and army to stop him. At Capua Sulla won a battle in what was becoming effectively a civil war. Two other generals marched their armies to support Sulla, Marcus Licinius Crassus

LITTLE BOOK OF **ANCIENT ROME**

and Gnaeus Pompeius. Riots in Rome led to the murder of several Sulla supporters, while Marius the Younger was elected consul and raised a new anti-Sulla army. The war reached a climax in vast battle fought outside the walls of Rome at the Colline Gate. More than 50,000 men were killed and Sulla emerged victorious.

Sulla entered Rome and had himself declared Dictator for Life. The office of dictator brought with it almost unlimited power, and had previously been used only as a temporary measure in dire emergency. He then began drawing up a list of men to be proscribed - meaning that they were executed and their property seized by the state. Within weeks around 1,500 patricians and equites had been killed, along with some 7,000 plebeians. One young man who managed to flee Rome in time to avoid execution was Gaius Julius Caesar, who was later pardoned after his influential relatives put pressure on Sulla.

Sulla then introduced a series of constitutional reforms which aimed to restore the power of the Senate, curb the power of the generals (such as himself) and set balances between the powers of different officials. Having got his package of reforms adopted, Sulla promptly resigned all his positions and retired to his country

estate to spend time with his family and write his memoirs. He died in 78 BC.

In 73 BC a group of gladiators broke out of their training school in southern Italy and precipitated a revolt by thousands of slaves. Led by the gladiator Spartacus the rebels plundered villas and farms, gathering numbers as they did so. The uprising was eventually put down by Crassus and Pompey, who chose to kill rather than take prisoners.

In 63 BC Lucius Sergius Catalina made a bid for power. He came from one of the oldest and most prestigious patrician families, but was himself poverty struck. He organised a plot among the rural poor to raise an army, march on Rome and assume power with a view to enacting some of the policies of the long-dead Gracchi brothers. However the plot was betrayed and the Senate was able to march an army against Catilina before he was ready. The resulting battle saw Catilina and most of his men killed.

In the wake of the Spartacus revolt, Catiline coup and successful wars in the East, a private deal was struck between the increasingly powerful and successful Crassus, Pompey and Caesar. They agreed that rather than compete power against each other, they would divide powers and positions between

themselves and their supporters. The agreement became known as the Triumvirate.

When news of the deal and the payment of huge bribes that put it into effect leaked out, many senators were appalled that the government of their country had been carved up in a private deal between three men. Opposition was led by the lawyer Cicero and the philosopher Cato. They demanded that everyone in public office obey the rules and the law.

The business of winning elections was becoming increasingly corrupt and expensive. As more and more Roman citizens moved into Rome itself they were increasingly able to go to vote, something that they had not been able to do so easily when farming their lands several days walk away. Those standing for election needed to gain favour from the huge numbers of plebeians, and so they resorted to all sorts of tricks and tactics.

LEFT Lucius Cornelius Sulla sought to preserve the power of the aristocrats in the Roman state and became dictator before suddenly retiring to his farm

ABOVE The battles won by soldier and politician Julius Caesar against the Celts in what is now France laid the foundations for his successful political career

BELOW A map of Gaul, the area inhabited by the Celtic tribes that were conquered for Rome by Julius Caesar

Some candidates laid on spectacular gladiator shows or wild animal hunts, handing out tickets only to those who had promised to vote for them. Others threw enormous parties at which the tables groaned with exotic foods and wines - all served free to those who voted the right way. Others hired gangs of thugs to beat up anyone who did not vote as instructed. Many noblemen employed plebeian citizens to work in their craftshops, on their farms or in other jobs - and expected them to vote for the employer's favoured candidate at election time. A few candidates resorted to straightforward bribes, paying cash to voters as they went to vote.

Gradually a vast series of networks of votes grew up. The relationship between a rich man and those who relied on him for jobs, financial support or free tickets to gladiator shows became one of the most important social links in Roman society. The rich man was termed the patron, the dependant man the client. Some patrons had thousands of clients on whom they could call. Some patrons could muster only a dozen or so clients, but they in turn were clients of richer men and as they could deliver more votes than just their own they could ask for greater favours in return.

Meanwhile Caesar had been made governor of three provinces in northern Italy and southern Gaul. He used the huge army this put under his command to launch a war of conquest against the Gauls, a Celtic people who inhabited what is now France, Belgium, the Netherlands and parts of Germany. Caesar defeated a number of wealthy tribes, confiscating money and goods in enormous quantities for both Rome and himself. His soldiers admired him and became his devoted followers.

Crassus had taken up an army command in the East and found himself at war with the powerful Parthian Empire. Crassus led an army of 40,000 men in an invasion of Parthia, which ended in disaster. At the Battle of Carrhae Crassus found his Roman armoured infantry outmanoevred by the fast moving and lightly equipped Parthian cavalry. With his supplies running out and with thousands of wounded to care for, Crassus accepted a truce from the Parthians, but when he went to negotiate a peace deal he was murdered along with most of his senior officers. The Parthians then stormed the Roman camp, killing 20,000 men and capturing 10,000 to be sold as slaves. A relatively junior officer, Cassisus, managed to rally some 10,000 survivors and fought his way back to Roman territory.

Pompey was meanwhile living in Italy and runnings things there with an efficiency and effectiveness that impressed everyone he met. The death of Crassus was followed swiftly by the death of Pompey's wife, Julia the daughter of Caesar. Then supporters of Caesar and Pompey came to blows in Rome in a series of riots that culminated in the burning down of the Senate House by Caesar's supporters. The Senate responded by calling on Pompey to restore order and instructing Caesar to disband his army and return to Rome.

On 10 January 49 BC Caesar gathered his army on the banks of the River Rubicon, now the Fimicino, which marked

BELOW A modern sculpture of Ambiorix, the Celtic chieftain who led resistance to Rome in what is now Belgium

ABOVE Bust of Marcus Junius Brutus

RIGHT The Roman commander Crassus was struck down from behind during peace talks with the Parthians

populares, who were led by Caesar. By 46 BC Caesar had won and Pompey was dead. But the cycle of bloodshed was not yet over.

Returning to Rome Caesar began a series of constitutional reforms that aimed to establish himself in power for the rest of his life and to give himself the right to appoint a successor. By removing all power from the elected officials and the electorate itself, Caesar made many enemies. Even though many of his social and legal reforms were highly regarded, his destruction of all pretence at democracy or senatorial prestige went against the grain of Roman culture and history. Some began to fear he would revive the ancient office of King of Rome for himself.

Two men organised a plot to murder Caesar. The first was the military hero Cassius, who had fought his way out of Parthia after the disaster at Carrhae. The second was the wealthy politician Brutus, whose ancestors had been instrumental in expelling King Tarquin from Rome and founding the republic. The men mustered much support from the Senate and from groups in the provinces whose influence was also threatened by Caesar's reforms.

the border between his provinces and Italy. When he marched his army over the river he precipitated another civil war between himself and Pompey. The war that followed revived the factions of the optimates, who backed Pompey, and the

On 15 March 44 BC Caesar was murdered when he want to a meeting at the Senate. The conspirators expected to be hailed as heroes for having killed a dictator and having restored the Republic, but instead they had to flee the city as Caesar's supporters rioted. Two of Caesar's key supporters, the general Mark Antony and politician Marcus Lepidus met to decide what to do next. They were joined by Caesar's youthful nephew and adopted son Octavian, who was named as Caesar's heir in his will. The three men agreed to keep Caesar's reforms in place, sharing the dictatorial powers between themselves.

The conspirators who had murdered Caesar may have had little support in the city of Rome itself, but they could count on support from rich men and local authorities in several provinces, especially in the East. There they mustered a large army and prepared to march on Rome. Mark Antony moved faster and with Octavian in support landed in Greece to attack first. At Philippi Antony won a crushing victory over Cassius and Brutus. Cassius was killed in the fighting, Brutus committed suicide soon afterwards.

Antony and Octavian returned to Rome in triumph where Lepidus had been running things in their absence. The

LITTLE BOOK OF **ANCIENT ROME**

three men then divided up the Roman world among themselves. Each of the men was allotted provinces to rule. Officially they were governors acting on behalf of the Senate of Rome, but in many ways they were independent rulers. Antony got the richest provinces in the East, plus Gaul. Octavian got Spain, Sicily, Corsica, Sardinia and other islands while Lepidus got the African provinces. Italy was given to the Senate to rule, but under the close eye of clients of the three men.

In 41 BC Antony met with Cleopatra, Queen of Egypt. At this date Egypt was the only powerful Mediterranean state that had neither been conquered by Rome

**LEFT** The death of Spartacus in battle ended the greatest of the slave revolts against the Roman government

**BELOW** A map of the Near East showing the provinces created by Rome after they conquered the region

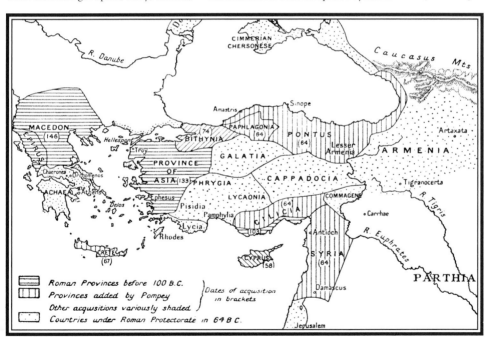

nor become an ally. Egypt was extremely rich and prosperous, but it lacked an effective army and was even more corrupt than Rome. Cleopatra saw in Antony and his ambitions an opportunity to ensure the survival of Egypt under her family's rule. She formed an alliance with Antony, promising him unlimited Egyptian money in return for military assistance. The two soon became lovers and had several children.

Octavian viewed Antony's alliance with Cleopatra as a threat. He thought Antony intended to become master of the entire Roman world. In 34 BC Antony had his children by Cleopatra crowned kings and queens at a ceremony in Alexandria. This Crucially made them rulers of Roman provinces of which he himself was governor. Octavian used this to convince the Senate and the vast majority of Roman citizens that Antony intended to strip Rome of the eastern provinces and give them to Cleopatra.

The Senate declared war on Egypt and put Octavian in command of the army sent to invade. Antony chose to muster his troops to support Cleopatra. After a naval defeat at Actium in 31 BC most of Antony's army deserted to join Octavian. As Octavian closed in on Egypt Antony committed suicide, followed by Cleopatra.

Octavian then returned to Rome. He set about reforming the constitution, as Sulla and Caesar had done before him. Octavian announced that he was going to restore the democratic constitution of the Republic. Outwardly this is what he did. The various officials were given back their old powers, the people were given back the right to elect whoever they wished and the Senate regained its old powers, prestige and rights.

Behind the scenes, however, Octavian kept supreme power in his own hands. He had the senate appoint him to be a proconsul, a protribune and a censor, giving him the powers of the three most important officials in the Roman state. He also took the power to decide who was able to put on gladiator shows, hold triumphal processions or organise free banquets. Taken together these powers allowed Octavian to influence who would win elections, and what actions they could take once they were elected. In practice Octavian rarely interfered directly with anything, but

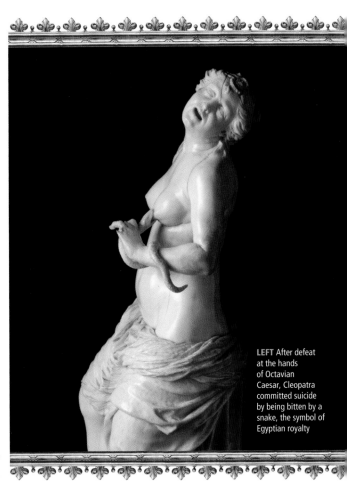

**LEFT** After defeat at the hands of Octavian Caesar, Cleopatra committed suicide by being bitten by a snake, the symbol of Egyptian royalty

wealth of that country to use in granting favours and handing out bribes. Secondly he got himself elected to be Pontifex Maximus, or chief priest, and had the Senate give him the title Augustus which gave him semi-divine status. He was now the richest man in the world and the most sacred, as well as the most politically powerful.

Although in many outward ways the democratic constitution of the Republic had been restored, the Republic was really dead. All power now lay with Octavian. From 27 BC onwards historians refer to the system of government begun by Octavian as the Empire, derived from another title he had given him by the Senate, that of Imperator. The Republic was gone, the Empire had arrived.

**ABOVE** Cicero sought to return democracy to the Roman constitution. He failed and was murdered on the orders of Mark Antony in 43 BC

**RIGHT** A coin showing the face of Cleopatra, Queen of Egypt

he did not need to do so. Anyone wanting to stand for election would first ask Octavian's permission, and once elected they took care not to do anything that would annoy Octavian.

To bolster his political power, Octavian took two other steps. First he made himself ruler of Egypt, giving himself the vast

## Roman Baths

The baths were a social institution in Rome. Everyone went to the baths to meet people, relax and enjoy themselves. As well as the cleansing baths, the buildings also included sports facilities and libraries. The main rooms were:

**Atrium** - Entrance hall

**Apodyterium** - Changing room with pegs for clothes to be left.

**Frigidarium** - Held a large pool of cold water for bathing and swimming. Workers here gave massages or sold food and drink to bathers.

**Tepidarium** - A room heated to be agreeably warm and lined with benches where people could sit and chat

**Caldarium** - A hot room with a basin of hot water which could be splashed over the bather's body

**Laconium** - A very hot room with wooden benches where people sat and sweated

## Roman Playwrights

**Livius Andronicus** - A Greek who came to live in Rome about 240 BC. He wrote versions of Greek plays in Latin.

**Plautus** - Born in the small town of Sarsina, Titus Maccius Plautus began his career as an actor but later wrote a series of comedy plays. He wrote his last play in 184 BC.

**Ennius** - Quintus Ennius wrote a series of plays about gods and heroes that included beautifully written poetry. He died in 169 BC.

**Terence** - Born in North Africa and taken to Rome as a slave in about 180 BC Publius Terentius Afer won his freedom by writing a number of comedy plays that delighted his owner.

**Pacuvius** - Marcus Pacuvius was best known as a painter, but his plays were also popular. He wrote serious works that explored ideas such as loyalty and treachery, love and hate, honour and disgrace. He died in 130 BC.

**Gaius Maecenas Melissus** - Apparently from southern Italy, Melissus wrote comedy plays about rich people behaving in foolish ways during the 1st century AD.

**Seneca** - Born in 4 BC Seneca wrote a number of tragedies, but he is better known as a philosopher.

# Chapter 5

# THE GLORY THAT WAS ROME

The new constitutional settlement made by Octavian, better known as Augustus after he acquired that title, remained in force for centuries. It would vary over the years as social and political circumstances changed, but essentially the system remained the same. The people voted in elections, the elected officials carried out their tasks and gained honour and prestige through their actions - but behind the scenes everything was manipulated and controlled by the Emperor.

After Augustus died in 14 AD his place was taken by his son-in-law and adopted son Tiberius Claudius Nero. Tiberius was a successful general and competent administrator. Under his rule the Roman Empire expanded again, taking in new territory in the Balkans, but he suffered defeat in Germany. In ad37 Tiberius died, leaving power to his great nephew Gaius Julius Caesar Germanicus, who was universally known by the nickname of Caligula, meaning "little boots". Aged only 25 Caligula was talented, popular and clever. His rule promised to be a high point for Rome, but within months of coming to power Caligula fell seriously ill. When he recovered he was a changed man - impulsive, vindictive and violent. He fell out with the Senate, executed men without trial and embarked on a lavish career of luxury and debauchery. On 22 January 41 Caligula was murdered by a group of young nobles.

Power then passed to Caligula's uncle,

Claudius who was also a nephew of Tiberius and a grandson of Mark Antony. It was Claudius who ordered the conquest of Britain, Judea, Lycia and Thrace. He made a point of getting competent men appointed to key positions, apparently so that he did not have to do much actual work himself. Under Claudius a vast number of roads, aquaducts and temples were built, as well as canals that he opened to the use of private merchants.

He also reformed the status of temples and priests, favouring native Italian deities over those from abroad.

The religion of ancient Rome was a mix of deities and spirits both from Rome and from other countries. Later Romans believed that in the very earliest years of the kings only eight deities were worshipped in Rome. However by the time of the later Republic there were dozens of temples in Rome to different gods, and many towns

ABOVE Nero was Roman Emperor from 54 AD to 68 AD and the last of the family of Julius Caesar to hold power. He was extravagant and took the Roman state to the edge of bankruptcy, though he remained popular with the people

taining a good relationship with the gods. This meant that it was important that the correct rituals and sacrifices were carried out properly and on time. The priests of the temples were responsible for carrying out these rituals, and for organising religious festivals throughout the year. The position of Pontifex Maximus, or chief priest, was an elected political office. The chief priest organised regular meetings of the other priests to make sure everyone was worshipping the deities in the correct way.

At first gods from outside Rome were brought to the city by people who moved to Rome and wanted to have a temple to their own gods to visit. Later on the Romans themselves began to worship gods from other countries. The gods of Greece were popular in Rome from about 200 BC, with Apollo and Diana being worshipped by vast crowds.

After about 50 BC what became known as mystery religions began to appear in Rome. The greatest of the mystery religions was the Eluesian Mysteries, which were centred at Eleusis in Greece. Once a year worshippers went to the Temple of Demeter at Eleusis and took part in rituals and ceremonies that were kept a closely guarded secret. Many richer Romans

or villages had their own local patron god as well. People were free to worship as many or as few gods as they liked. Some people visited different temples at different times of the year or if events happened in their lives.

The Romans believed that they owed the success and wealth of Rome to main-

ABOVE Modern re-enactors recreate a review of Roman troops by an emperor in the later 1st Century AD

went to Eleusis, but the rituals were not carried out at Rome.

Rather different was the religion of Mithras. This Persian god was worshipped in underground temples where men gathered to take part in secret rituals. These rituals seem to have included sacred re-enactment of events in the story of Mithras and a special meal that seems to have consisted of wine, roast beef and bull's blood. There were seven grades of initiate in the worship of Mithras, with the ranks bearing no relation to the social status of the man who held it. Inside a Temple of Mithras a slave might rank higher than a nobleman.

Dionysus was a Greek god of wine and agriculture, but he also headed a mystery religion. The rituals of this mystery were open to both men and women. The rites are not entirely clear, but they certainly involved drinking enormous quantities of

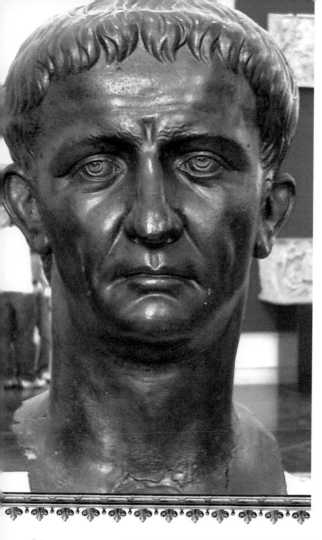

wine and prolonged dancing to a rhythmic drumbeat as well as the sacrifice of a goat. At first the devotees of Dionysus went out into woods to perform the rituals, but by about 30 BC the rituals took place inside temples.

It seems to have been these mystery religions that Claudius disliked. He felt that the concept of performing religious rites in secret went against the ancient Roman tradition of worshipping the gods openly so that everyone could ensure the worship took place properly.

It may have been this dislike of secrecy that turned many Romans against another new religion from the East that began to appear in Rome about the year 50 AD: Christianity. The early Christians met in houses to remember Jesus Christ and carry out rituals such as baptism and mass. Another reason for Roman hostility to the Christians was that they refused to worship other gods. Since the Romans believed that the well being of the state and people depended on the proper worship of the gods, anyone who refused to take part was seen as an enemy of the state. In time Christianity would gain in strength and would eventually become the official religion of Rome, but under Claudius it was viewed with hostility.

In October 54 AD, Claudius died after a sudden illness. There were rumours he had been murdered, but this was never proved. His place was taken by his adopted son and actual great nephew, Nero. The emperor was young and dashing. He spent large sums on public entertainments and was especially fond of the fine arts such as theatre, music and painting. He managed to defeat the Parthian Empire and negotiated a peace deal that lasted for generations. Nero also oversaw the defeat of the rebellion of Boadicea (or Boudicca) in Britain.

In July 64 AD, in the middle of a hot dry summer, a fire broke out that devastated central Rome. Nero was in Antium at the time singing a song as part of a stage performance. When a messenger rushed in with news of the fire, Nero sent orders to muster men to fight the blaze, then went back on stage to finish his song. This incident later entered legend, with Nero being portrayed as behaving in a heartless way by singing a song and playing a lyre while Rome burned. Nero himself blamed the Christians for the disaster and ordered several of their leaders to be executed - including St Peter and St Paul.

Despite his efficient administration and artistic policies, Nero was not popular

## Types of Gladiator

**Hoplomachus** - Wore a helmet and small round shield, fought with spear and sword

**Laquearis** - Wore no armour, fought with a lasso and dagger

**Murmillo** - Wore a helmet, armguard and army-style shield, fought with army sword

**Provocator** - Equipped like a Roman legionary

**Retiarius** - Equipped with an arm guard, fought with net and trident

**Samnite** - Equipped like a Samnite soldier

**Secutor** - Wore a helmet and rectangular shield, fought with a sword

**Thraex** - Equipped like a warrior from Thrace with helmet, square shield, leg armour and short, curved sword

LEFT Claudius ruled the empire from 41 AD to 54 AD. It was during his reign that the conquest of Britain was begun

## The 8 Gods of Royal Rome

**Jupiter** - King of the gods and god of the kings
**Mars** - God of war and peace
**Quirinus** - God of battles
**Minerva** - Goddess of wisdom, medicine and commerce
**Juno** - Goddess of marriage and childbirth
**Ceres** - Goddess of grain crops
**Liber** - God of freedom and civic rights
**Libera** - Goddess of the plebeians

**RIGHT** A soldier of the later Roman army. He has armour made of toughened leather and a round shield that were lighter, though not as effective as the earlier metal armour and oblong shield. He has two javelins plus a long sword and a dagger

bodyguard marched out on him Nero realised all was lost and had a servant kill him. Months of chaos followed, but eventually an army general named Vespasian marched into Rome. He used his troops to force the Senate into granting him all the rights, privileges and powers that had been given to Augustus and so became Emperor of Rome.

The death of Nero marked a turning point in the Roman Empire. The family of Julius Caesar was now extinct and the army had shown itself to be capable of deciding who would be emperor, and who would not. The army was not all powerful, however. The Senate still had great influence, as did the voting citizens and richer noblemen. For decades to come the political history of Rome would be dominated by emperors seeking to balance the competing claims of Senate, people and army while fighting off barbarians, dealing with the Parthians and keeping law, order and prosperity flourishing throughout the Empire.

The fighting core of the Roman Army at this date was the Legion, a body of men that was to acquire a permanent form and

with the army. He rarely visited the troops, never led campaigns in person and very often diverted money intended to pay the troops to other projects. In March 68 AD the legions stationed in northern Gaul rose in revolt over pay issues. Other legions joined the rebellion and marched on Rome. Nero ordered men he thought loyal to come to his aid, but none came. When even his own

real unity very different from the legions of earlier years.

Each legion was a permanent formation with its own full time officers, armourers and supply system. Each legion was also given a sacred standard in the form of an eagle mounted on a pole to symbolise the pride and unity of the organisation. The legions were given numbers to identify them and their men.

Recruitment to the legions was still, officially, through an annual muster of eligible citizens. In practice, however, an increasing number of soldiers served for years at a time. At first - under Marius - this was something of a vague and open ended commitment. The state would hire the men annually, mimicking the original yearly muster, and the men would sign on for a year at a time. By the time of Vespasian, however, longer term contracts were introduced and a service period of 25 years had become standard.

The increasingly long lengths of time that soldiers spent in the Legions made it impossible for them to maintain a farm or business during their service. Those who survived their years in the army would need some way to earn a living on their retirement. It therefore became standard for a retiring soldier to be given a small

holding, or the cash to buy an inn or shop, on his discharge.

The men were organised into maniples, a unit of 160 soldiers led by two centurions, one senior to the other. Each centurion commanded a century of 80 men. Each century was divided into 10 units of 8 men each, who shared a tent, cooking pot, rostered duties among themselves and were led by a decurion. In most circumstances, however, a group of three maniples worked together both on the battlefield and for administrative purposes such as

ABOVE A scene of a gladiator combat in which the central figure is surrendering to the man wearing a closed helmet

**RIGHT** Roman soldiers work a ballista that can throw a bolt over 600 metres

**FAR RIGHT** A legate issues orders to his officers, their rank shown by the plumes on their helmets

**BELOW** A legate watches a parade along with officers and a standard bearer

THE GLORY THAT WAS ROME

pay and supplies. This unit was termed a cohort, ten of which formed a legion.

Each man in the legion was equipped identically, the standardisation being made possible by the state paying to equip each recruit on his enrolment, though the soldiers were responsible for maintaining their equipment thereafter. The details of the weaponry varied over time, but all the men were sent into battle as heavy infantry.

Most legions had about 120 mounted men on their strength, but these were not fighting cavalry. The mounted legionaries acted as scouts for the legion and dispatch riders for the officers. They were not expected to form up as cavalry units in battle, that job was given to specialist mounted units recruited for the purpose.

It was the centurions who maintained discipline and good organisation in the new army. They worked in pairs, each pair commanding a maniple and were responsible for keeping their men in fighting trim, ensuring equipment was up to specification and for delivering their units to the battlefield in a fit state to fight. In each legion one centurion was appointed to be senior over all the others. This man, the primus pilus or

'first spear', carried out the administrative duties of the legion.

Ranking above the centurions were the tribunes, usually six serving in each legion. These men came from the richer families of Rome. Some were serving permanently with a legion as a career choice, others served for only a year or two to gain experience in the army before opting for a career in the civil service, in politics or simply returning to the family estates. Although socially far superior to the centurions many tribunes were content to take the advice of their inferiors when it came to professional matters.

Above the tribunes were the Prefects, only two or three serving in each legion. These men were as socially privileged as the tribunes but tended to be exclusively full time

## The 12 Great Gods of Imperial Rome

**Jupiter** - King of the gods and god of the sky.

**Juno** - Queen of the gods and goddess of marriage and childbirth

**Neptune** - God of the sea and of horses

**Minerva** - Goddess of wisdom, medicine and commerce

**Mars** - God of war and peace

**Venus** - Goddess of love, beauty and prosperity

**Apollo** - God of music, poetry and the arts

**Diana** - Goddess of animals and wild places

**Vulcan** - God of blacksmiths, fire and volcanoes

**Vesta** - Goddess of the home and family

**Mercury** - God of travelling, messages and luck

**Ceres** - Goddess of agriculture and grain crops

LITTLE BOOK OF **ANCIENT ROME**          99

## Famous Roman Roads

**Via Appia** from Rome to Apulia, built 312 BC

**Via Aurelia** from Rome to Marseilles, built 241 BC

**Via Flaminia** from Rome to Rimini, built 220 BC

**Via Raetia** from Verona over the Brenner Pass to Germany

**Via Agrippa** network in Gaul linking Lyon to Marseilles, Cologne and Amiens, built 13 BC

**Ermine Street** from London to York, built 96 AD

**Fosse Way** from Lincoln to Exeter, built 49 AD

**Watling Street** from Dover to Caerleon by way of London and Wroxeter, built 47 AD to 120 AD

soldiers. They usually had distinct duties and responsibilities. The Prefect Castrorum, for example, was responsible for the construction and organisation of a fortified camp whenever the legion halted in enemy territory.

Commanding the entire legion was the Legate. Unlike the majority of the men and officers in the legion, the Legate was a temporary appointment. Few Legates served with a particular legion for more than a year or two at a time. They were appointed by the Consuls and were almost invariably men close to and loyal to the Consul who appointed them.

Rome's legions were full time professional organisations. It was this professionalism that made them so effective in battle. As the men were serving full time

for many consecutive years it was possible to train them to a degree of skill impossible in part time soldiering which was the norm in other states and societies in those days.

When a Roman citizen joined a legion the first thing that he did was to take an oath of loyalty to "the Senate and People of Rome". The initials of these words in Latin were SPQR and were carved into the stonework of army buildings throughout Roman territory and stamped on military equipment. There was no doubt about who was in charge. Having taken his oath, the new recruit was assigned to a maniple.

The second thing that a recruit had to do was learn to march. The battlefield manoeuvres expected of a legion were many and complex, but they all depended on the men marching at the same speed as each other. This, in turn, meant that each man had to take strides of identical length in step with all the other men, a technique known as the 'legionary pace'. A new recruit spent hours each day pounding a parade ground until his centurion was content that he would keep to this legionary pace, even in the stress of battle. Only then did he progress to more advanced training.

Having acquired the legionary pace,

FAR LEFT Legionaries of about 100 AD in marching order (left) and parade dress (right)

LEFT An auxiliary cavalryman recruited from a Celtic tribe

BELOW A camp scene from about 100 AD. The tent is made of leather

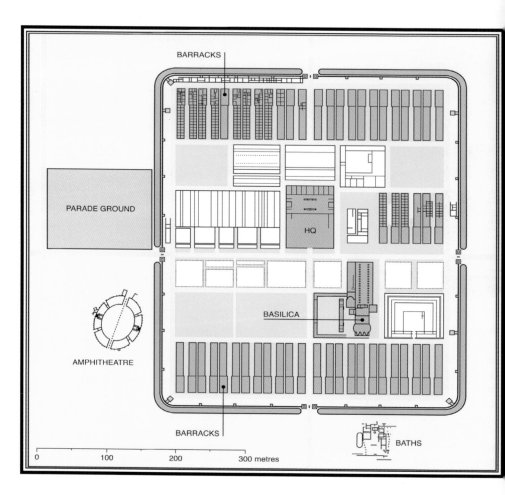

BARRACKS

PARADE GROUND

HQ

AMPHITHEATRE

BASILICA

BARRACKS

BATHS

0    100    200    300 metres

the recruit had to learn formation marching. Columns six men abreast were the standard for distance marching, but battlefields demanded men marching in unison dozens or hundreds of ranks deep and files abreast. Sudden alteration of direction needed to be carried out faultlessly.

The parade ground of each legion included an area in which were planted thick wooden posts as tall as a man. These were used for sword training. Armed with a shield and sword, the recruit would learn to jab with the point of his sword, not slash with its edge. The short sword, or gladius, was short and broad with a slight indent near the hilt. Most men carried a short, pointed dagger as well as a sword. Although it could be used as a weapon, this dagger seems to have been used more often as a personal knife for cutting food, working leather and other domestic chores.

LEFT A diagram showing the layout of a typical Roman military base. Similar designs were used for towns and in some places can be traced to the present day

ABOVE A group of German barbarians who have joined the Roman army return home on leave

ABOVE The Roman
assault on Anglesey in
60 AD was resisted by
the local Celts, urged
on by druids
and priestesses

Equally important was the ability to use the shield for offensive as well as defensive purposes. A sudden blow with the shield could be effective at stunning an enemy.

The second standard weapon of a legionary was the pilum, a throwing spear with a long metal shank and stout wooden haft. These had to be thrown with some accuracy over a distance of 50 yards or more. During training the sharp point of the pilum was covered in leather padding to minimise accidents. The iron shank behind the point was designed to bend on impact so that it could not be thrown back. As an added measure the wooden pegs that held the shank to the wooden handle were made so thin that they would snap as the pilum hit its target.

Even though their main role was to fight on foot in formation, legionaries were trained to perform a variety of tasks. They were all expected to be able to ride a horse and to swim. Each legionary was expected to be able to dig field fortifications and to know how to dig pits of the right width and depth to trip a charging horse.

The rounds of training took place every morning and afternoon for recruits and continued day after day until his centurion was satisfied. Thereafter the recruit was put through the usual daily exercises of the legion, which included weapons drill and formation marching lasting several hours.

A key feature of army routine was the regular long distance route march. A daily march took place, but the main essential was a march of about 20 miles which took place once every 10 days or so. Everyone in the legion, without exception for age, rank or duties, had to take part in this march.

The men were also taught skills that would prove to be invaluable on campaign. They learnt how to forage for food for themselves or the horses and how to light a fire and keep it burning. For camping duties the men were divided into groups of 8. These men shared a tent made of leather, a metal cooking pot and, when possible, a mule to transport the gear. This division of men into eights to care for their daily needs was an ancient one that went back to the Royal Army when heavy infantry in the phalanx drew up for battle eight ranks deep.

The standard formations of the Roman army laid down a standard formation for a legion on the march. The order of march was designed to ensure that the legion could cover as much ground as possible without becoming disordered and while able to respond to sudden emergencies, such as the need to repair the road or fend off an enemy attack.

Ideally the Legate would know where he was going, either having a map or a set of written instructions on how to reach his destination. If this were not possible a local guide would be hired to show him the way.

The first troops to move forward would

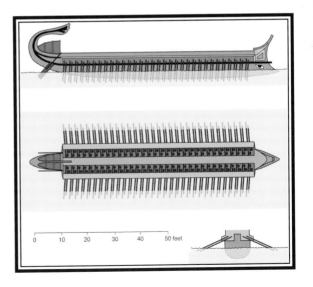

BELOW The Roman navy of about 100 AD used long, thin galleys powered by oars to fight pirates or barbarian raiders

be the cavalry, sent out in small groups to ride well in advance of the legion. Their main task was to scout the route ahead. In friendly areas the main problems would be obstacles, such as broken bridges or poor road surfaces. If any such were found the scouts would send gallopers back to summon engineers to effect repairs. In enemy territory the dangers of ambush could be very real. Cavalry scouts would investigate any potential ambush sites, but would not be expected to tackle the opposition, merely to keep an eye on the enemy while messages were sent back to the Legate.

The first unit of the column proper was a cohort of infantry formed up for battle. Wearing full armour and carrying their weapons ready for instant action this was often the First Cohort. In enemy territory these men had to be ready to respond instantly to messages sent back by the scouts, but would also be the first into action if the enemy managed to launch a surprise attack. Even in friendly country this forward unit marched in armour, though helmets were sometimes slung from a shoulder strap.

Behind the leading cohort came a mixed group made up of one man from each of the groups of eight men who camped together. These men had the task of marking out the camp at the end of the day, erecting tents and getting cooking fires lit. When mules or donkeys were available, each man would be leading one to which were strapped the tents, cooking pots and other camping equipment.

Next in the order of march came the engineers with their picks, shovels and other tools. Ready to repair roads, build bridges or carry out whatever other task was demanded of them, the engineers included carpenters, armourers, builders and blacksmiths.

Behind the engineers came the commanding officer, the Legate. He usually rode a horse on the march and was accompanied by a small escort of mounted officers waiting to carry his orders and instructions along the column or ride off with dispatches to nearby towns or other army units. The personal baggage of the Legate and his officers was usually kept next to them in the line of march.

Immediately behind the officers came the engines of war. The catapults, ballistas and other heavy equipment were usually dismantled for the march and loaded onto wagons. It might take several hours, even a couple of days to assemble these weapons, so they usually used only in major battles or sieges, not in skirmishes.

Also loaded into wagons were the bulk supplies of the legion such as flour, grain, bacon, spare weapons and horseshoes. It was the speed of these heavy weapons that determined the pace of the column. An ox cart moves at about 2.5 miles per hour and can cover some 17 miles each day, though the ox soon tire and need to be rested about one day in four.

The main strength of the legion came behind the dismantled heavy weaponry and bulk supplies. Headed by the sacred eagle standard, pay chest and other valuable items the men marched six abreast. The width of most roads was constructed to cope with such a column of men. Behind the cohorts of marching men came the remainder of the cavalry, often riding some distance behind the column to ensure that no enemy could sneak up from behind to launch a hit and run raid.

Although this standard formation was

ABOVE In 101 AD the
Roman Emperor Trajan
invaded the wealthy
kingdom of Dacia, now
Romania, and earned
the love of his men by
his care for them. On
one occasion he tore his
own cloak into strips to
use as bandages

adopted by most legions in most circumstances, there were variations in the field.
In open country the legion might form up
in three columns, each marching abreast
of the others, so that the legion formed a
more compact body. In wooded country
the cavalry would be pushed out on either
side of the column as well as in front and
behind in an attempt to flush out any
enemy lurking in the trees. If a legion was
needed in a hurry it might leave its heavy
weapons and baggage behind to speed up
the rate of march. Conversely, if a legion

were moving its permanent base it would
need to transport vast quantities of para-
phernalia including bathing equipment,
soldiers' wives and children, household
effects. A marching legion could resemble
a small mobile city.

A significant piece of military wear was
the caliga, the marching sandal. The up-
pers were made of a network of narrow
straps which tied together over the foot
and around the ankle. The sole was made
up of several layers of leather and shod
with a mass of iron studs. The health and

hygiene of the soldiers' feet was of paramount concern in an army that depended on marching for its mobility and its success. In colder climates the sandal was lined with fur or cloth to improve warmth.

As the caliga was important to marching ability, so was another item of equipment important to self sufficient mobility. This item was the T-shaped wooden pole which legionaries slung over the shoulder and from which was hung their personal kit. Earlier armies had loaded equipment on to wagons when on the march, but the Romans prized the speed and mobility of its armies. Each man was therefore expected to carry his personal effects including drinking cup, blankets, three days of rations, entrenching tools and spare clothing. Only the tent and cooking equipment shared by a group of eight men was carried separately by a mule. The sight of these heavily encumbered men on the march earned the legionary the nickname of "mule"

Helmets followed a pattern copied from the Gauls around 150 BC. Neck flap and cheek pieces guarded against blows to the sides and back of the head, and a strip of metal, rather like a short peak, stuck out from the front of the helmet to provide added strength to the area that would take

the force of an overhead slashing blow, but without adding much weight.

The main body could vary. Under the Republic and early Empire it consisted of a sleeveless mail tunic reaching to about mid-thigh length. Officers, in contrast, adopted the Greek style body armour known as the muscled cuirass. This consisted of solid plates of metal, usually bronze, on the front and back of the body. These plates took their name from the fact that they were moulded to resemble the muscular torso of a naked

ABOVE A modern copy of the statue of the god Jupiter which stood on the Capitoline Hill in Rome. The eagle was the symbol of Jupiter and in his right hand he holds the goddess Victory

North Sea, Baltic Sea, NIJMEGAN, NEUSS, BONN, MAINZ, STRASBOURG, Rhine, REGENSBURG, LORCH, VIENNA, BUDAPEST, IGLITA, BELGRADE, Danube, Black Sea, ARCAR, SILISTRA, Adriatic Sea, Tyrrhenian Sea, Aegean Sea, Mediterranean Sea

Fortified wall
Major fortress
Fort

0   250   500   750 kilometres
0         250        500 miles

ABOVE The system of forts, garrisons and strongpoints that the Roman built along the Rhine and Danube rivers to keep the barbarians of central and eastern Europe out of the Empire

and thighs were covered by metal studded leather straps that dangled down from a belt.

The shields of the period were also gradually evolving. Before about 100 BC the most popular shape for the large, curved scutum had been oval. This style was replaced by the time of Claudius by a more oblong shape, though the corners continued to be rounded. By the time of Vespasian the shield had completed its transition to a rectangular shape. At the same time it was found that the plywood composition which gave the shield its combination of lightness and strength was vulnerable to the cold damp encountered campaigning in northern Europe. A bronze rim was added around the shield to help prevent damp seeping in to the wood and waterproof leather covers were produced to protect the shields during rain.

Greek hero. Badges of rank came in the form of ornamental belts. By around 100 AD, however, a new style of body armour called the lorica segmentata came in. This was formed of several strips of steel that curved about the body or over the shoulder and were laced together to encase the body from waist to shoulder. The hips

The legions were supplemented by a

much larger number of auxiliaries. These were troops raised from the provinces and composed of men who were not citizens of Rome. These men were not paid as well as the legionaries and were frequently used to bear the brunt of any fighting by commanders reluctant to send back long lists of dead Roman citizens after a battle. Many auxiliary units were equipped with the weapons and armour of their own locality. Thus Gauls were often raised as cavalry with mail shirts, small oval shields and long swords designed to slash down at a man on foot, while the Numidians of North Africa formed units of unarmoured, fast-moving cavalry which showered an enemy formation with javelins thrown from the horse at the gallop. One key reward the auxiliary soldier could look forward to after his years of service ended was to become a Roman citizen.

ABOVE In 271 AD the Alemanni, a confederation of southern German tribes, invaded northern Italy but were defeated at Pavia by the Emperor Aurelian who met their leaders to impose peace terms and take hostages

A wall painting dating to around 50 AD found at Pompeii that shows the goddess of love, Venus, in the arms of the god of war, Mars

The Roman armies were trained to fight, but fighting was not all that they did. Having a huge standing army of around 400,000 fit and active men gave the emperors a useful pool of manpower. The soldiers were called upon to carry out a large number of construction projects. Some of these were for military use - forts, defensive walls and roads among others - but some were for civilian use. The troops were also used for purposes that today we might consider the task of police and civil servants. Soldiers enforced the decisions of judges, carrying out executions and mutilations or guarding prisoners condemned to slavery.

Rome was now rich and powerful beyond the dreams of its founders. Almost the entire civilised world around the Mediterranean belonged to Rome. To the south lay the vast Sahara Desert, to the west was the Atlantic, to the north various barbarian tribes and to the east the wealthy, powerful and hostile Parthian Empire. There would be wars against Parthia and the barbarians, but the dominance of Rome was not to be seriously threatened for centuries.

Within the Empire, Rome held a dominant and commanding position. Free men could be citizens of their own city or country - be it Athens, Egypt or Marseilles - but only citizens of Rome could be elected to high office, take part in legal cases or enjoy tax exemptions. Gradually at first, and faster later on, the numbers of Roman citizens expanded as citizenship was granted as a reward for service in the army or in local government. By around 300 AD all free, adult men in the Empire were citizens of Rome, though slaves and women could not be citizens.

# Great Roman Festivals

### 15 February
## Lupercalia

The city was purged of evil when two goats and one dog were sacrificed at the Cave of Lupa. Whips were made from the skins of the sacrificed animals and given to two young men who had the blood poured over them. The men then ran through the streets whipping any women they could reach.

### 17 March
## Liberalia

Boys who had become 14 in the previous year were declared to be adult men. After a feast at home the boys joined a procession that marched around the city calling at 27 sacred shrines and temples.

### 7 June
## Ludi Piscatori

A festival in honour of the god of the River Tiber. Fish caught from the river were burned on the altar of the Temple of Vulcan. Everyone in Rome had the day off work.

### 6-13 July
## Ludi Apollonares

A week-long festival to honour the god Apollo. The theatres put on special shows while horse and chariot races took place in the Circus Maximus.

### 23 July
## Neptunalia

A festival in honour of the god Neptune that involved horse racing. Also a day on which elections were held.

### 28 August
## Sol Luna

A festival honouring the sun and moon with chariot races and other events in the Circus Maximus.

### 5-19 September
## Ludi Romani

The games honouring the god Jupiter. A great procession through the streets was followed by chariot racing, horse racing, athletic contests, theatre shows, gladiator fights and feasting.

### 15 October
## October Horse

This festival honoured the god Mars. It began with a procession to the Campus Martius, a field north of the city where the army traditionally practised. Chariot races took place and the lead horse of the winning team was killed using the sacred spear of Mars. The severed head of the horse was then nailed to the walls of Rome.

### 17 December
## Saturnalia

This festival began with a procession to the Temple of Saturn, followed by sacrifices. This was followed by people giving each other gifts and by feasts and parties held in private houses. Traditionally slaves had the day off work and gambling was allowed within the walls of the city.

# Chapter 6

# THE FALL OF ROME

After the year 300 the Roman Empire went into a long decline. The reasons for this change in fortunes have been debated long and hard by historians, and by the people who lived through the turbulent and violent years. Nobody has ever really come to a secure conclusion as to the reasons.

The reasons for the decline and fall of Rome were various and complex. Among the long term causes was a change in the climate of Europe. The weather was gradually becoming cooler and wetter. This made it more difficult to grow the corn and other crops on which people then depended for food. More people than before had to spend time working in the fields to grow food, which meant that there were fewer people around to work as soldiers, priests and government officials. However, the men who occupied positions of power did not want to see a cut in their standards of living, so they imposed heavier taxes on the farmers and workers. This led to a slow economic decline that meant that there was even less money available than before.

The Empire was also suffering from a fall in the population. In the year 250 a new disease struck the Roman Empire and caused a massive death toll. At one point 5,000 people a day were dying in Rome alone and it is thought that as much as 20% of the people in the Empire may have died over a period of 10 years. The disease seems to have come from Africa and though the ancient authors did not

describe the symptoms very well it may have been the first time that smallpox occurred in Europe.

The changing climate and outbreaks of disease led to economic and social problems. The Emperor Diocletian blamed the problems on the fact that the growing number of Christians refused to worship the traditional gods. He unleashed a persecution of Christians in the year 303. Churches were destroyed and the Chris-tian church stripped of its wealth. Anyone who refused to sacrifice to the gods was to be punished. Most people were fined or sacked from their jobs, but Christian leaders were sent to the their deaths. Some were thrown alive to starving lions as the Romans believed that to be killed by an animal was deeply dishonourable. It is not clear quite how many people were killed but it is likely around 7,000 died.

The persecution was called off after

a few years, but it left a legacy of distrust and hostility between Christians and pagans. When the Christian Constantine I became Emperor in 324 AD it was the Christians turn to burn down temples, seize wealth and execute their opponents.

To deal with the growing crisis, successive emperors concentrated more and more power in their own hands. The roles of the Senate, elected officials and local nobles were increasingly undermined. Elections still took place and the Senate still met, but real power lay in the hands of officials appointed by the Emperor. The result was that the government became increasingly unable and unwilling to deal with real problems affecting the mass of the population of the Empire. Officials instead obeyed orders from the Emperor and his court since their own promotion and careers depended on pleasing the Emperor, not the people.

By the year 350 the tax system had been changed so that the bulk of tax money raised was paid direct to the Emperor. Local towns and cit-

ies were no longer able to keep most of the money they raised themselves and spend it locally on roads, canals, aquaducts and other useful purposes. The money went to the Emperor who spent it on the army, lavish living and lost it in corruption, which became progressively worse. Nor could the local authorities afford to enforce law and order, so in many areas bandits and robbers became common, while pirates prowled along the coasts. An

indication of how bad corruption had got comes from Gaul in 362 AD. A local governor cracked down on corruption, sacking dozens of tax collectors and launching an investigation of who paid what and where the money went. Within a year the amount of money paid by local farmers fell by a third, although the money sent to the emperor stayed the same.

As the inhabitants of the Empire struggled under increased taxation, falling

LEFT Atilla the Hun leads his savage hordes of barbarians into Gaul in 451 AD. The Huns slaughtered hundreds of thousands of people as they looted wide swathes of territory and did enormous damage to the ability of the Roman Empire to survive

ABOVE In 410 AD the Visigoths invaded Italy. Although less violent than some other barbarians, the Goths looted widely and forced Romans to act as their servants

RIGHT A Goth in battle kit. The unusually shaped shield is typical of the Goths as are the two, light throwing javelins

wealth, declining population and religious troubles they grew less and less inclined to join the army. The Emperors turned to men from outside the Empire, especially Germans, to fill the ranks instead. Some barbarians were enrolled into the Roman army and treated as if they were Romans. Others were hired as complete units, often serving under their own king who was paid cash for a set period of time. Another way to raise fighting men was to move a barbarian tribe into the Roman Empire and give them farmland left vacant by the falling population in return for serving as soldiers for a set number of days each year. This system of employing barbarian soldiers solved the problem of recruiting men to the army, but left the Emperor vulnerable to rebellions and desertions.

As the 4th century progressed attacks by barbarians over the Rhine and Danube became increasingly frequent. A key factor in this was that a new barbarian people had surged into Europe from the East - the Huns. Swarming out of the Asian steppes, the Huns fought on horseback using bows and swords. They moved fast, slaughtered without mercy and withdrew back to Asia with alarming speed.

In 378 the Goths, a Germanic people, defeated and killed the Emperor Valens in the Battle of Adrianople in the Balkans. The Romans lost about 10% of their army in the battle, which proved to be a catastrophic blow. German barbarians swept over large areas of the empire to loot and kill.

By this date the Roman Empire had been divided into two. A Western Empire consisting of Gaul, Italy, Britain, Spain and most of North Africa was ruled by emperors who were nominally based in

Rome but who in practice spent most time with the army on the barbarian frontier. The Eastern Empire consisted of Greece, the Balkans, Egypt, and the Middle East and was based in Constantinople (now Istanbul). The two emperors were supposed to co-operate with each other, but often fought each other in bitter wars that cost the Empire men and money it could not afford to lose.

Not only was the empire divided into East and West, but civil wars became increasingly frequent as generals and nobles squabbled over the diminishing wealth. One of the most damaging of these wars began in 383 when the general Magnus Maximus defeated the Picts and Scots in northern Britain. His victorious troops hailed Magnus Maximus to be Emperor, and were duly rewarded with huge sums of cash. Magnus hurriedly recruited barbarian mercenaries to guard the borders of Britain, then took his army to Gaul. The troops in Gaul joined the rebellion, gaining their own cash reward. When the Western Emperor Gratian led an army into Gaul to put down the rebellion he was killed and his army slaughtered. In 384 Magnus set out to march into Italy, but stopped at Milan when he learned that the Eastern Emperor Theodosius I

had sent a large army to Rome to make Gratian's younger brother Western Emperor as Valentinian II.

For the next three years Magnus ruled Gaul, Spain and Britain, but then he invaded Italy again and drove Valentinian II out of Italy. Theodosius I sent a new army to the West which defeated Magnus at Save. Magnus summoned reinforcements from Gaul, but was defeated and killed at Siscia. Meanwhile the Franks had poured into Gaul, delighted to have a free hand for plundering while the defending troops were away in Italy fighting a civil war.

The civil war fought by Magnus Maximus had cost the lives of tens of thousands of soldiers, and many more civilians. The damage done to the defences of Britain and Gaul were never properly repaired, and the economy of Gaul was devastated by the Frankish incursion. It was but one civil war of many fought at this time.

When Valentinian II died in 392

BELOW A Hunnish warrior. The Huns preferred to ride into battle and were highly skilled at shooting arrows from a galloping horse, something that bewildered the Roman armies they faced

AD the commander of his army, Arbogast, grabbed power. This Arbogast was a red-headed Frank who had been hired by Theodosius as a mercenary commander and had been instrumental in defeating Magnus. As a barbarian, Arbogast could not be emperor himself so instead he persuaded the Senate to appoint a nobleman named Eugenius to be Western Emperor. Arbogast then travelled north to agree a peace treaty with the Franks and other Germanic peoples.

Back in Rome Eugenius had reopened the pagan temples and although he did not persecute the Christians, he did strip the church of lands and wealth that it had taken from the pagan temples. Pope Siricius, Bishop of Rome, was outraged and appealed to the Christian Eastern Emperor Theodosius for help. Theodosius mustered an army and invaded Italy in 394. Once again the armies of the two halves of the Roman empire slaughtered each other. Arbogast and Eugenius were killed and Theodosius installed his son Honorius as Western Emperor.

Honorius was only 11 at the time, so real power rested with his talented military commander Stilicho. Stilicho was half-barbarian as his father was a Vandal, but he gained Roman citizenship from his mother's family and joined the army. He rose rapidly to high command and was greatly trusted by Theodosius. Stilicho was an energetic commander, he defeated a rebellion in North Africa, crushed a Pictish invasion of Britain and drove the Goths out of the Balkans. But in 395 AD the Huns themselves arrived, rampaging through Syria, Armenia and nearby areas before they withdrew back to Asia. The damage done was immense and so sapped the strength of the Eastern Empire that Stilicho knew he would get no help from the east.

In 402 AD King Alaric of the Visigoths invaded northern Italy and although he was defeated at Pollentia by Stilicho, he retreated north with his army intact. Three years later the Germanic Alans, Sueves and Vandals invaded Italy. Stilicho again drove them out but the financial and military resources of the Western Empire were by this date becoming exhausted.

In 406 AD the barbarians driven out of Italy crossed the Rhine into Gaul. The Roman commander in Britain, Constantine, declared that Stilicho and Honorius could not cope. He declared himself Emperor and called on the troops in Gaul to support him. Some did, some did not and yet another civil war broke out. Alaric the Visigoth chose this moment to threaten to march into Italy. Stilicho bought him off with a huge cash payment so that he could concentrate on the war against Constantine, but this alienated the Senate and Honorius. In circumstances that remain murky, Stilicho was killed by troops loyal to Honorius.

Hearing that Stilicho was dead and no longer able to command the Roman armies, Alaric led his Visigoths back into Italy. They poured south, looting and raping as they went before they finally ended up in front of the walls of Rome itself. The vastly impressive Aurelian Walls were too strong for the Visigoths to storm, so Alaric laid siege.

ABOVE A Frankish warrior with his typical small round shield and long lance. The francisca throwing axe is tucked into his belt

**ABOVE** The Aurelian
Walls of Rome were built
around the city in 271 AD
by the Emperor Aurelian
after German raiders had
reached northern Italy.
They run for 19km, enclose
14 sq km and were perhaps
the strongest defensive
walls in the world

**RIGHT** The siege of Rome in
537 AD saw Goths seeking
to break into the city by
attacking the Mausoleum
of Hadrian, which the
defenders had made
into a fortress

and many of his men were Christians so the churches were largely left alone and civilians were killed only if they tried to stop their houses being looted.

The sack of Rome in 410 AD was a turning point. The great city had stood inviolable since the occupation by the Gauls 800 years earlier, and even then the Capitoline Hill had withstood attack. Never before had the entire city fallen to enemy attack, but now it had.

Tens of thousands of Romans left the city. Some moved to live with relatives in nearby towns or villages, others moved to North Africa which had so far remained safe from barbarian attack. The population nosedived. Where over a million people had lived in the days of Augustus there were by 425 AD only 90,000 and after a second sack by the Vandals in 455 AD it went down to half that.

Alaric died soon after he captured Rome and his Visigoths moved to southern Gaul where Honorius granted them lands and self-government as the price for peace. But peace there would not be. Constantine was defeated and killed in 411 AD, but other generals rebelled in Gaul, Spain and North Africa.

Beset by these troubles, Honorius found himself faced by a request by the

He sent messages to Honorius offering to retreat in return for cash payments, but Honorius refused to pay. Nor would Honorius send an army to help Rome.

After some weeks starvation set in among the people of Rome and the situation was getting desperate. At dawn on 24 August 410 AD a group of Gothic slaves opened the Salarian Gate and let Alaric and his army into Rome. For three days Alaric allowed his men to plunder, loot, kill and rape. As sackings go, however, Alaric's sack of Rome was remarkably restrained. Alaric

rities of Britain asking him to appoint a governor to take over from the man appointed by Constantine, who had been ousted. Unable to do anything else, Honorius told the British to elect one of themselves as a temporary stopgap measure until he had defeated the rebellions and the barbarians and could send a new governor to Britain. Nothing more is heard of the British province in Roman records, and Britain slipped into the Dark Ages.

Back in Italy Honorius died in 423 AD leaving no legitimate children. He was succeeded by his nephew Valentinian III. The new emperor set about reforming the administration of the Western Empire, or what was left of it. He sought to deal with the Germanic invaders by recognising them as governors of provinces they had conquered in return for payment of taxes. The ploy worked in places, giving the new barbarian rulers legitimate control at the cost of loyalty to Valentinian. Elsewhere the move failed. In Spain King Hermeric of the Suebi accepted his appointment of Governor of Gallicia and promised to pay taxes to Valentinian and send troops when required. Hermeric never paid anything nor did he send troops, other than to loot neighbouring parts of Spain.

In 451 AD the Huns under their king

Attila invaded Gaul, then moved into Italy in 452 AD. Both times they were driven off, but only after killing tens of thousands of people and inflicting massive damage on farms and towns.

In 455 AD Valentinian ordered the summary execution of the general Aetius, and was soon afterwards murdered by troops loyal to the dead commander. The Senate proclaimed a wealthy senator named Petronius Maximus to be Emperor, but he was in turn murdered by a mob just 11 weeks later. Another senator, Avitus, then took over as emperor but he died the next year in murky circumstances.

The next emperor, Majorian, was a capable general and skilled civilian administrator. In other circumstances he might have achieved much for Rome, but it was too late. To much territory had been lost to barbarian rulers, too little taxation was coming to Rome and corruption had too firm a hold.

The Roman Empire had become a failed cause. Farmers found that barbarian kings took less in taxation than did Roman governors. In many cases the new rulers did not ask for taxes at all, but instead asked the farmers to work for them a few days a year. With the climate getting even worse it was better for farmers to work a few days for a barbarian who lived locally and whom they knew than to pay money to a distant emperor who frittered the cash on corruption and never did anything to help.

Majorian's reforms threatened to reduce the wealth of landowners in Italy, to stop the flow of tax money into the pockets of corrupt officials and to end the employment of barbarian mercenaries. On 7 August 461 AD he was murdered

BELOW A map of the Roman Empire as it was in 400 AD showing the routes taken by the principal barbarian tribes that invaded, conquered and destroyed the Empire

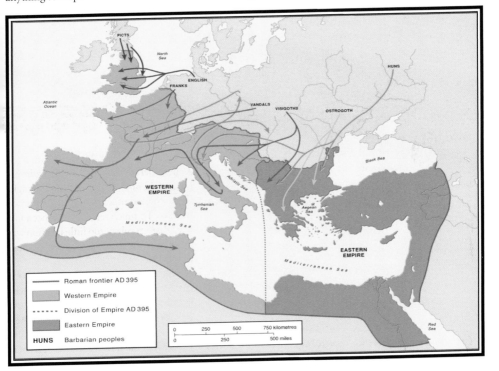

PICTS

North Sea

HUNS

ENGLISH

FRANKS

Atlantic Ocean

VANDALS VISIGOTHS OSTROGOTH

Black Sea

WESTERN EMPIRE

Adriatic Sea

Tyrrhenian Sea

Aegean Sea

Mediterranean Sea

EASTERN EMPIRE

Mediterranean Sea

Red Sea

| | Roman frontier AD 395 |
| | Western Empire |
| - - - - | Division of Empire AD 395 |
| | Eastern Empire |
| **HUNS** | Barbarian peoples |

0   250   500   750 kilometres

0   250   500 miles

**ABOVE** As the Western Roman Empire collapsed into chaos and destruction, the Eastern provinces were held together by Leo I who ruled from 457 AD to 474 AD. Many credit him with having transformed the Eastern Roman Empire into the Byzantine Empire that would survive until 1453.

he died in 465. The Eastern Emperor, Leo I, moved fast and sent a successful general and nobleman named Anthemius to be Western Roman Emperor.

Ricimer welcomed Anthemius for the men he brought with him to fight the barbarians. The two men worked well together for a while, but then fell out in 470 AD when Anthemius put a friend of Ricimer on trial for treason. Riots followed and Anthemius took refuge in St Peter's Basilica on the Vatican Hill. Leo sent the general Olybrius to Italy to support Anthemius, but Olybrius immediately changed sides and with Ricimer stormed St Peter's and killed Anthemius.

Olybrius then became emperor and sent a message to Leo asking for his support and recognition. The move was a shrewd one by Ricimer and may have led to peace with Leo. But Ricimer died in August and Olybrius in October, both apparently from natural causes. Ricimer's place as head of the Germanic mercenaries who now almost exclusively composed the army of Rome was taken by his nephew Gundobad while Leo sent another general to be emperor, Glycerius.

Neither man lasted long. Leo I died in Constantinople and the new emperor, Leo II, replaced Glycerius with Julius

on the orders of the commander Ricimer, a Suevi prince who had taken service as a mercenary of Rome.

As a barbarian Ricimer could not be emperor, so he followed the lead of Arbogast and appointed a Roman senator to be Emperor instead. As emperor Libius Severus did what he was told but

Nepos. Glycerius retired gracefully and later became Bishop of Milan. Gundobad, meanwhile, left Rome voluntarily when his father died and he inherited the throne of the Burgundians. Just how low the Western Roman Empire had fallen is shown by the fact that Gundobad preferred to rule a small barbarian people than be head of the Roman army.

Taking over the reins of office, if not of power. Julius Nepos chose a half-barbarian general named Orestes to take over from Gundobad as head of the army. Orestes promptly returned the favour by deposing Nepos and bundling him off back to Constantinople. As the emperor, Orestes chose his own son who was a Roman citizen through his mother and the grandson of a noted senator and nobleman. He was installed with the imperial titles in October 475 AD.

The new emperor's name was Romulus and he was given the title of Augustus. He thus bore the name of the first King of Rome and the title of the first Emperor of Rome. If that seemed auspicious it was not to be.

The German mercenaries rose in rebellion over a pay dispute. They were led by a man named Odoacer, about whose background little is known. Orestes was killed in a skirmish at Placentia and Odoacer caught up with Romulus Augustus at Ravenna. Odoacer peremptorily told the 12 year old boy to hand over the insignia of his official positions, to resign all power and to become a humble private citizen. Romulus Augustus did as he was told, and was rewarded not only with his life but also with a generous pension and an escort of soldiers to take him to his relatives on his mother's side who owned land in southern Italy.

Odoacer contemplated the imperial regalia that lay in front of him. He sent them to the Eastern Emperor, Zeno, in Constantinople along with a message saying that Rome no longer needed an emperor. Odoacer declared himself to be King of Italy instead.

In Constantinople Zeno tried to save face by taking the title of Western Emperor for himself and giving Odoacer the title of Patrician of Rome, with permission to rule Italy on Zeno's behalf.

Nobody was fooled. The Roman Empire was dead and gone.

ABOVE A soldier of the later Roman Army. He is armed with a long, thrusting spear and his shield has a Christian symbol painted on it

Design & Artwork: ALEX YOUNG

Published by: DEMAND MEDIA LIMITED

Publisher: JASON FENWICK

Written by: RUPERT MATTHEWS